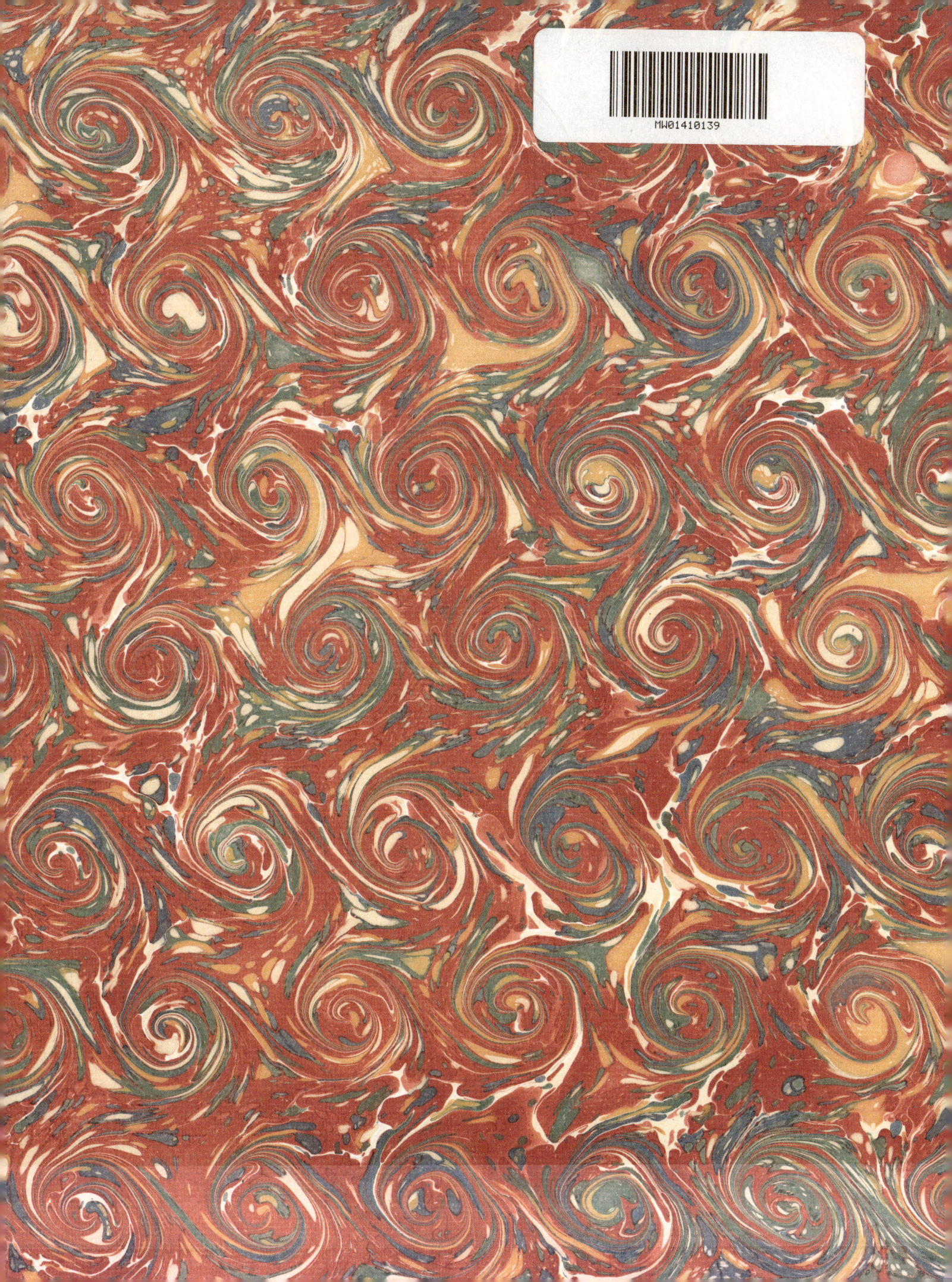

CHINOISERIES

For Alan Salz

First published in the United States of America in 2008
by Rizzoli International Publications, Inc.
300 Park Avenue South
New York, NY 10010
www.rizzoliusa.com

© 2008 Bernd H. Dams and Andrew Zega

All rights reserved. No part of this publication may be reproduced, stored in a retrieval system, or transmitted in any form or by any means, electronic, mechanical, photocopying, recording, or otherwise, without prior consent of the publishers.

2008 2009 2010 2011 / 10 9 8 7 6 5 4 3 2 1

Printed in Singapore

ISBN-13: 978-0-8478-3046-6

Library of Congress Catalog Control Number: 2007938545

Chinoiseries

Bernd H. Dams & Andrew Zega

Foreword by Hubert de Givenchy

RIZZOLI
NEW YORK

Contents

Foreword by Hubert de Givenchy

11

Authors' Note

13

I. The Architecture of Joy

14

II. "A Graceful Disorder"

54

III. Sir William Chambers

92

IV. Georges Le Rouge

130

Selected Bibliography

160

Illustration Credits

162

Opposite: A Chinese Costume, *watercolor by Louis-René Bouquet.*

Foreword

Since their first exhibitions in Paris, I have followed the path of Andrew Zega and Bernd H. Dams, and during certain of these exhibitions I was able to acquire several very beautiful drawings that they created. Each time their themes renew themselves in a marvelous way—be they pavilions, statues, fountains or grottoes.

Their latest work on Chinoiserie pavilions and pagodas, of which I have just had a preview, is among their most successful, especially as most of their chosen models have sadly disappeared. And of course it is a joy to be able to admire afresh the conception of their work and its particular elegance.

These precious documents retrace an epoch when taste, extravagance and a sense of fantasy were an essential part of the way in which parks and gardens were embellished, by perfectly inscribing them in nature, then furnishing them with dreams.

The continuing research of these two great artists enchants me as much as the perfection of their precious drawings.

With these few lines, I am very happy to tell them how much I admire them and how much I thank them for bringing to life an era when imagination, luxury and beauty had their say.

Hubert de Givenchy

Authors' Note

THIS BOOK REPRODUCES forty-two of our watercolors of Chinoiserie pavilions. Several works were originally published in our first book, *Pleasure Pavilions and Follies*, and one, the Porcelain Trianon at Versailles, in our third, *Palaces of the Sun King*. They are included here because the purpose of the present volume is to gather the entire body of our historical work in this most remarkable architectural style, spanning more than fifteen years of activity.

All these structures are in some way exceptional—either aesthetically or historically—and we have not attempted to be encyclopedic; our selection is, if anything, representative rather than systematic. Though Chinoiserie pavilions were found throughout Europe and America, French examples overwhelmingly predominate, just as France dominated the style, with hundreds of pagodas erected in the last decades before the Revolution—a happy confluence of the focus of our research with that country's architectural patrimony. Figures are at times eloquent, and two-thirds of the structures presented here were constructed or designed in the decade from 1775 to 1785, the fevered apex of France's Chinoiserie mania.

We should also mention a few points concerning the watercolors themselves. The buildings are presented in architectural elevation—a scaled representation of the main façade depicted without perspectival distortion. There is no common scale among the drawings. The color schemes of certain pavilions are interpretations, based on examples found in documents and the decorative arts of the period; when historically accurate we note this in the accompanying descriptions. Likewise, certain decorative details are also interpolated, necessarily due to the imprecision of period representations. A roof, for example, may have been made of lead sheets and not slate shingles, or vice versa. Details such as this, for what were considered minor buildings, have simply been lost to time.

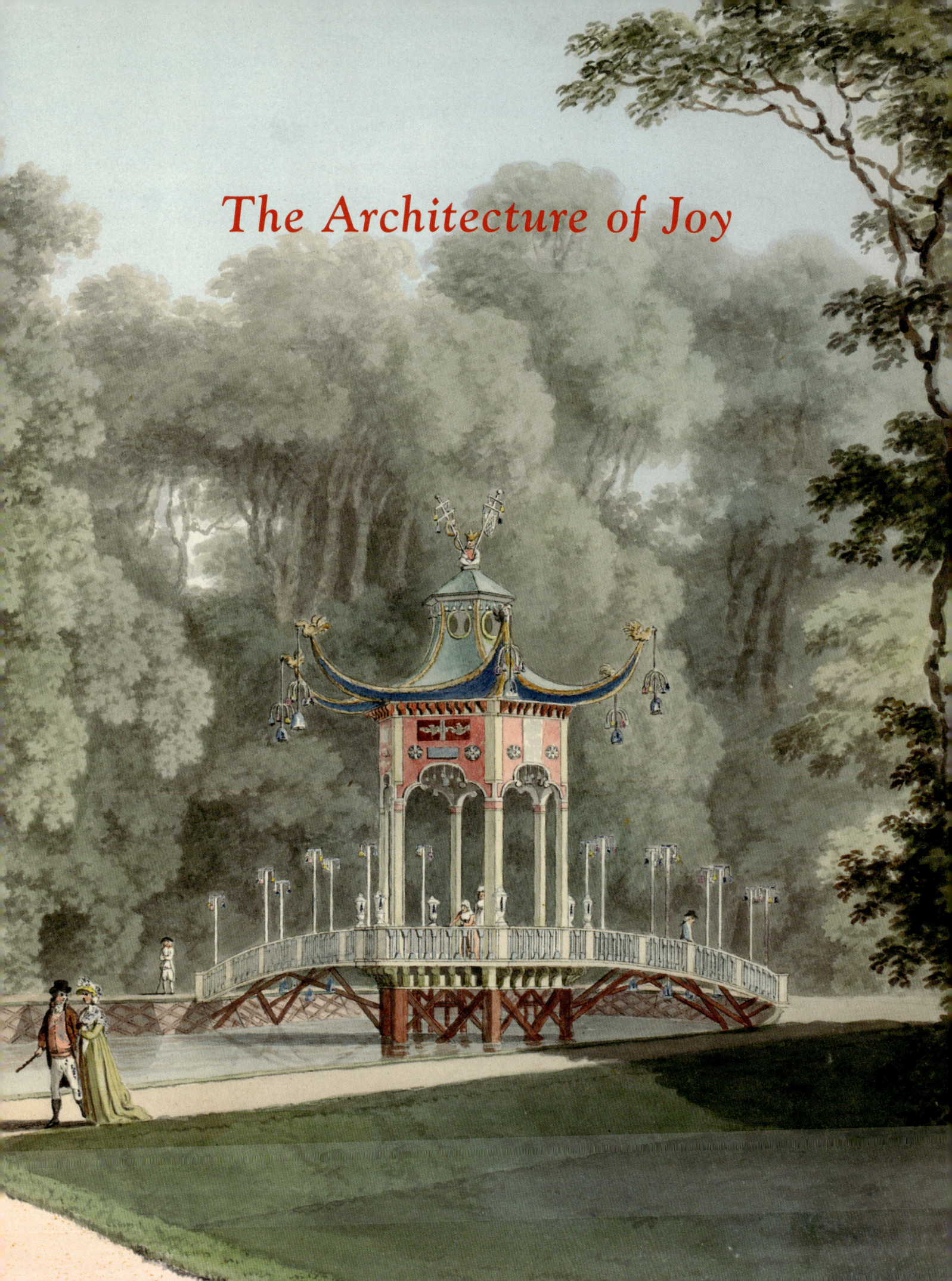

The Architecture of Joy

Previous pages: the Chinese Bridge at Laxenburg (p. 143), *watercolor by L. Janscha.*

The Architecture of Joy

Let us begin with an example. The pagoda at Rosay (*p. 156*) stands atop a large, finely made grotto, so large that a dozen people can—and once surely did—dine in the vaulted cave beneath. An iron hook is embedded in the center of the vault to hold a chandelier, and discreet shelves and niches have been worked into the writhing rock to hold lanterns, food and beverages—doubtless roasts, wine and champagne. Water from springs on the hillside above has been channeled in lead pipes underground to spout from crevasses, tumble over the tortured rock and collect in rustic basins that feed the pond in which the grotto stands. The pagoda above is reached by a bridge of finely wrought iron that springs from a densely planted hillock and arches gently over water to the grotto. Inside, the floor of limestone slabs is set with cabochons; the walls are wainscoted with scagliola and a faux-marble frieze supports a sky-blue vault.

It is possible that four people could also dine in the pagoda, its dozen diamond-glassed French doors thrown open on a summer evening, and this too must have occurred a number of times in the two centuries and more since it was built, but dining in the pagoda and the fact that it has an interior at all seem superfluous when inside it; musty, aged, uninhabited and uninhabitable, the interior is an afterthought, and one wants always to be outside, the better to look at the building itself. The pagoda at Rosay is a unique survivor, the last Chinoiserie pagoda in France to stand on its grotto in a park retaining its original landscape and follies, facing its château, an ensemble complete and essentially unchanged from the time of the Revolution. Rosay is a time machine.

To visit Rosay is to understand why our forebears, its builders, often bankrupted themselves creating gardens and inhabiting them with fantastic structures. Remove the highways, the television, the whole of modern life and a folly in one's

Chinoiseries

garden becomes an inexhaustible source of delight. Looking then at Chinoiserie in eighteenth-century Europe, a time itself synonymous with grace, and attempting to describe the structures themselves—fretwork pagodas and brightly painted summerhouses set atop rockwork grottoes—such nearly anachronistic words as whimsy, charm and delight immediately spring to mind. And no wonder, for Chinoiserie is Western architecture's equivalent of plain, simple joy. Even today a pagoda, well done, cannot but elicit a smile.

Apparently it was always so. From their first meaningful awareness of its existence, Europeans were intrigued by China, and this fascination would only grow with the centuries, fueled on the one hand by a trickle of fantastic tales and superbly worked luxuries and on the other by the land's seductive aloofness. From the outset, two Chinas developed in the European mind; knowledge of one, the actual country, came fitfully, with long periods of self-imposed isolation compounded by many misconceptions and outright deceptions, but the other, the imaginary world of Cathay, was a pure invention, a collective vision nurtured, embroidered and beloved by the European spirit. As Hugh Honour explains, "Chinoiserie is a European style and not, as is sometimes supposed by sinologists, an incompetent attempt to imitate the arts of China…Cathay is, or rather was, a continent of immeasurable extent lying just beyond the eastern confines of the known world. Of this mysterious and charming land, poets are the only historians and porcelain painters the most reliable cartographers."

It was Marco Polo's *Travels*, first disseminated in 1295, which brought China to the attention of medieval Europe and first inspired the mythic land of Cathay. Though his account would be validated by historians centuries later, his

The Architecture of Joy

contemporaries, befuddled by descriptions of an empire vaster, better governed and wealthier than even ancient Rome's—a prosperous, highly civilized world beyond the hostile barrier of Arab lands—seemed to have read his book as a work of fiction. Marco Polo recounted his story with wide-eyed wonder, and thanks to the talent of his collaborator, the romance writer Rustichello di Pisa, he painted prose pictures of compelling drama and enchantment. His description of the Kublai Khan's palace at Chandu, reached after a long and eventful journey, could, with but minor alterations, have been written four centuries later by a visitor to the Sun King's Versailles:

> *There is at this place a very fine marble Palace, the rooms of which are gilt and painted with figures of men and beasts and birds, and with a variety of trees and flowers, all executed with such exquisite art that you regard them with delight and astonishment. Round this Palace a wall is built inclosing a compass of sixteen miles, and beautiful meadows, with all kinds of wild animals… In the Park where there is a charming wood he has built another Palace built of cane, of which I must give you a description. It is gilt all over, and most elaborately finished inside. It is stayed on gilt and lackered columns, on each of which is a dragon all gilt, the tail of which is attached to the column whilst the head supports the architrave. The roof, like the rest, is formed of canes, covered with a varnish so strong and excellent that no amount of rain will rot them… The Palace is so devised that it can be taken down and put up again with great celerity; and it can all be taken to pieces and removed whithersoever the Emperor may command. When erected, it is braced against mishaps from the wind by more than two hundred cords of silk.*

Chinoiseries

Chandu lay at the very heart of Cathay, and the evocative power of Marco Polo's artless poetry would prove so potent that more than five centuries later it inspired Samuel Coleridge to dream the gilded pleasure dome of Xanadu, the greatest literary ode to this fabled dominion. Much closer in time to Polo himself, the witty imposter Jean d'Outremeuse, also inspired by Marco Polo's work, concocted *The Travels of Sir John Mandeville*, and it was this dazzling medieval fabrication—a realm of fantastic monsters and wealthy sages residing in golden halls beneath ceilings encrusted with precious stones—that became what could be called anachronistically Europe's first best seller and that, with Marco Polo's account, jointly laid the imaginative foundations of Chinoiserie.

Concurrently Chinese porcelain and decorative arts began to reach Europe, imported via the ancient trading routes of the Silk Road. Coveted by aristocratic collectors, these extraordinary objects held pride of place in their curiosity cabinets long before they became near-commodities in the eighteenth century. Despite their rarity, Chinese objects were merely considered remarkable curios, decorative and perhaps even mystical, but in no way valued for any ethnographic information they might hold, and from its inception to its decline, Chinoiserie's most defining characteristic would remain the confluence of fantasy and opulence.

The discovery of a sea route to the Orient popularized and ultimately democratized the taste for Chinese porcelain and decorative arts, and the Portuguese were the first to hold the lucrative trade monopoly. Their efforts, the first truly global trade, rendered this small nation the wealthiest in Europe and King Manuel I the

Opposite and following page: The Chinese Empress and Emperor, *by Bernard Rode.*

The Architecture of Joy

richest man in the world. The Portuguese trading empire reached its zenith with the establishment in 1557 of a commercial stronghold at Macao, where inexpensive export wares were bought to be resold with shocking profit throughout Europe. However, Portugal had neither the logistical infrastructure nor the military might to defend these exceedingly long shipping routes and the rising maritime power of the Netherlands assumed their monopoly at the end of the sixteenth century.

Venetians dabbled in the production of Majolica wares *alla porzellana* and in the 1570s Grand Duke Francesco I de' Medici established a short-lived factory to create faux porcelain, the so-called Medici Porcelain, but it was the Netherlands that succeeded in creating faïence imitations at Delft, their astounding financial success in turn inciting the creation of factories at Nevers, Rouen, Nuremberg, Fulda and Bayreuth, all of them striving to produce imitation Chinese porcelain for an insatiable European market.

By the mid-seventeenth century, fueled by growing demand for all things Chinese, authentic or not, sinomania began to influence the decorative arts in the Netherlands, England and France. Concomitantly, the reports of Jesuit missionaries, the Counter Reformation's proselytizing vanguard, were profoundly shaping the European vision of China and influencing European thought. In 1585 Pope Gregory XIII confided both China and Japan to their mission, despite the bitter protest of other Catholic orders, and the Jesuits became the dominant evangelical force in China as well as China's most eloquent advocate in the West. The Jesuits' utopian vision of China as a sophisticated society guided by superior morals and Confucian logic was to exert a strong appeal across the intellectual landscape of Europe, and though the encyclopedists of the Age of Reason implicitly mistrusted

Chinoiseries

them, manifold convergences between Confucian theories of government and the ideals of the Enlightenment are traceable to Jesuit influence. Both insisted that the only justification for the existence of government is to provide peace and happiness for its citizens and that good governance must be founded on actions that do not contradict the nature of the human mind. These actions are reasonable only if they are virtuous and thus ensure the common welfare. Arbitrary government is illegitimate by simple application of virtue and logic.

Such ideas were rightly judged dangerous in an age of divine right, and the Bourbon dynasties of France and Spain increasingly found the Jesuits intolerable irritants. Nor did the Jesuit society help its cause with its protector the Church; their stipulation, based on Eastern thought, that the highest degree of societal morality was founded upon the purity of natural law was a subversion of fundamental transcendental dogmas. Under mounting pressure from the Bourbon courts, Pope Clement XIV reluctantly suppressed the Society in 1773. It was of course an act of desperation, far too late in coming to squelch the order's influence: Voltaire and Diderot were both Jesuit pupils.

Two influential illustrated books from the 1660s, Athanasius Kirchner's *China Monumentalis Illustrata* and John Nieuhoff's report of the Dutch embassy to the Manchu court, together became the late seventeenth century's encyclopedia of China. Both offered extensive descriptions of the country, its government and society, but their impact overwhelmingly resided in hundreds of engravings—the first apparently authoritative illustrations of the fabled Cathay. However, the visual content of both books was often a deception: scenes were naïvely drawn and thoroughly un-Asian, lacked relevant detail and a number were outright fabrications.

The Architecture of Joy

Nieuhoff's guileless plates were so influential that even fifty years later Johann Fischer von Erlach, in his *Entwurf einer Historischen Architektur* (1721), closely followed his architectural precedents, further cementing European misconceptions of China. Nieuhoff's iconic view of the Nanking Tower (*p. 119*) would serve as the blueprint for Chinoiserie garden follies for generations to come, just as his description of the Tower's red, green and yellow palette became their color template. European travelers became so familiar with these illustrations that upon arrival in China they would invariably ask directions to Cathay, unable to believe that what they saw was indeed their destination. Ironically, this very artlessness rendered these Western misrepresentations immediately comprehensible, further stimulating a burgeoning interest in China—or more precisely, its European interpretation.

In what was by then a well-established dynamic, by the late seventeenth century the simple scarcity of reliable information, induced by the new Manchu dynasty retaining a policy of self-willed isolation inherited from its Ming predecessor, again acted to untether China from reality. Europeans projected the winsome fantasy of Cathay into this void, inspired by the tall tales of Eastern adventurers and their own imitation trinkets. Disparate, often conflicting accounts simultaneously claimed authority, and the confusion and opacity they generated were compounded by the completely alien nature of Chinese thought—the key to understanding that remained obscure and tantalizingly beyond reach. Quite simply, China in all spheres stood in diametrical opposition to the European consciousness of the baroque age, rendering it a virtual cipher. "I come straight from Congo," the character of a Chinese doctor announced upon entering a Parisian stage in 1692.

Chinoiseries

26

The Architecture of Joy

Though export porcelain and scroll paintings offered numerous authentic depictions of Chinese architecture—pagodas and tiny huts scattered about the countryside, often in the distance—Europeans, when they came to build their own Chinoiserie follies, simply ignored their precedent. Likewise the Chinese concept of the picturesque, the "graceful disorder" of Sharawadgi defined by William Temple in *The Gardens of Epicurius* in 1685, was completely foreign to the Baroque sensibility and would have little impact on the design of European gardens until well into the next century. "Their [the Chinese] greatest reach of imagination is employed in... contriving figures, where beauty shall be great, and strike the eye, but without any order," Temple wrote presciently, without the least indication that any reader, in an aesthetic world ruled by symmetry, had taken notice.

Though lacquer-paneled rooms and porcelain cabinets were by then no longer rarities, Chinoiserie first established itself as a style in interior decoration in Baroque France, and paradoxically much credit must be given to Louis XIV. A protean figure dominating Europe for half a century, he both shaped the tenor of his time and planted the seeds for its overthrow. He and his court's fascination with the exotic found ample expression in numerous court festivities, in costumes and in the ephemeral decorations for his youthful *divertissements*. Typical was the Carrousel of 1667, where the king appeared disguised as a Chinese emperor, to great acclaim. The highly influential Porcelain Trianon at Versailles (*p. 31*), though it was the earliest example of Chinoiserie architecture erected in Europe, predating the first examples built in Germany by well over forty years, was essentially

Opposite: A Chinese Tent *by Jean-Baptiste Pillement, engraved by J. Deny and C. Leviez.*

Chinoiseries

Rocks in the forest of Fontainebleau, by Georges Le Rouge, Les Jardins Anglo-Chinois à la Mode.

a compound of sober classical pavilions garbed in a Baroque fantasy of Chinese décor—the interior brought outside.

Ostensibly a pleasure pavilion dedicated to the indulgence of the senses, the Trianon was also a cipher for France's universal political ambitions, where Louis XIV, allegorical Emperor of the East, signaled his intention to displace the Netherlands from its dominance of Eastern trade. Predictably, it incited many imitators and the name "Trianon" became synonymous throughout Europe with a pleasure pavilion in a garden setting. However, none of Trianon's imitators imitated its Chinese ornamentation; rather, the Chinoiserie décor of the Sun King's Oriental folly would exert its influence inside, stimulating a Parisian fashion for blue-and-white Chinoiserie interiors *à la Trianon*.

The Architecture of Joy

The Orient also held sway in fashion, and throughout the reign nothing was considered more exotic than dressing up in Oriental costumes for court masquerades. The new century opened with the elaborate festivities of *Le Roy de la Chine* on January 7, 1700, such a success that it was reprised at Marly the following day. Only a few months earlier the Duchesse de Bourgogne, wife of the king's grandson and heir to the throne, had urgently demanded the services of her confessor, the Jesuit Father le Comte, an eminent intellect and author of the recently published *Nouveaux mémoires sur l'état présent de la Chine.* Fearing spiritual crisis, the curé rushed to her apartments; receiving him, the duchess dismissed his entreaties after her soul with a laugh and instead demanded he design an authentic Chinese costume for her to wear to a court ball.

    With the Régence, Antoine Watteau, Claude Gillot and François Boucher imagined a universe of cavorting monkeys and parasol-toting mandarins floating on scraps of earth, sheltered by festive tents and Seussian pagodas, tethered by garlands and ribbons to gilded rocaille boiseries. In time Chinoiserie's gestation in interior décor would transmute into the rococo, all the while gathering and absorbing the most diverse influences until the predilection with Cathay finally spread out-of-doors and developed into an architectural style. Jean-Baptiste du Halde's *Description de l'Empire de la Chine* (1735), one of the most popular books of its time, was instrumental in diffusing this new sensibility. Its imaginary scenes, often with buildings as a backdrop, encapsulated the playfulness of the rococo, both stimulating and embodying the ambivalent longing for another world.

Porcelain Trianon at Versailles

Louis XIV, commissioner
Charles Le Brun and François d'Orbay, architects
built 1671
destroyed 1687

Demolished after standing but sixteen years to allow construction of the Grand Trianon in its place, the Porcelain Trianon nonetheless remains a veritable legend. Its five pavilions, erected in a fantastic Oriental style and set amid intimate flowering parterres, were conceived as a youthful monarch's pleasure dome—a world apart where Louis XIV could, for an afternoon, escape Versailles and its etiquette, his own constricting creations.

Though the first Chinoiserie building in Europe, the Porcelain Trianon nonetheless has little stylistically of the Orient about it, other than the blue-and-white color scheme of its heavily ornamented mansard roofs and the riot of vases lining its balustrades and roof crests. In fact, if one caches its roof, the Royal Pavilion is a sober classical building. All construction plans are lost, leading to the legend of the Trianon's unparalleled expense and its porcelain-tiled roofs, though both misconceptions have a certain basis in truth. Close study of the royal accounts and period engravings has led us to believe the compound's roofs were actually lead sheets sculpted in bas-relief and painted to resemble porcelain—a major program of embellishment undertaken two years after the compound's initial construction.

Chinoise at Oggersheim

Friedrich Michael von Zweibrücken, commissioner
Paul Egell, architect
built circa 1755
destroyed

Set on an elevated slope and offering sweeping views of the surrounding countryside, the Chinoise at Oggersheim was designed by the architect Paul Egell in the mid-1750s for the Prince Friedrich Michael von Zweibrücken. Contemporary with Bruchsaal's Indian House (1754) and the Chinese Tea House of Frederick the Great at Sans Souci (1754–1756), the belvedere at Oggersheim is a fine early example of the exuberance of German Chinoiserie, which combined the graceful lines of rococo architecture with decorative elements characteristic of Chinoiserie's imaginative style, most prominently palm corner columns—completely foreign to Chinese architecture—and the dragon surmounted by a mandarin holding an umbrella, symbol of enlightened rule.

The palm tree, symbol of King Solomon's Temple and emblem of wise government, was employed as an architectural ornament predominantly in Germanic countries. As late as 1774, the French royal architects Antoine Richard and Richard Mique would rely on this Germanic vocabulary when proposing Chinoiserie follies at Trianon (*pp. 39, 41, 73*), though the style was rendered outmoded upon the publication of Chambers' *Design of Chinese Buildings* in 1757.

Pagoda at Rheinsberg

Prince Heinrich of Prussia, commissioner
Frechhelm the Elder and Langner, architects
designed circa 1765
destroyed

Though his life was spent in the shadow of his older brother, Frederick the Great, Heinrich of Prussia was recognized throughout Europe as one of the most accomplished figures of the Age of Enlightenment. Like Frederick, Heinrich was a passionate amateur gardener, architect and philosopher, and competed with him for public acclaim. Contemporary visitors agreed that the gardens of his residence at Rheinsberg, some sixty miles north of Berlin, outshone those at Potsdam through their remarkable layout and the encyclopedic depth of thought lavished upon the numerous follies. Though they were foremost decorative eye-catchers, follies also invoked distant lands and philosophies, and at their best served to encapsulate the world's cultures during an afternoon's promenade.

Following his brother's example at Sans Souci and that of his sister Ulrike, Queen of Sweden, at Drottningholm, Heinrich designed the ultimate German rococo pagoda for Rheinsberg. The octagonal structure—its corners accentuated by gilded palm trees—was surmounted by an incurving roof painted yellow and decorated by colored bands. Gilded putti caryatids, intimations of Prussian Classicism, supported the upper, bell-shaped roof, which was crowned by a gilded mandarin, symbol of political wisdom and enlightened rule. Like the king's Chinese tea house at Sans Souci, the pagoda served as an idiosyncratic salon for Heinrich's famed gatherings of artists, philosophers and writers.

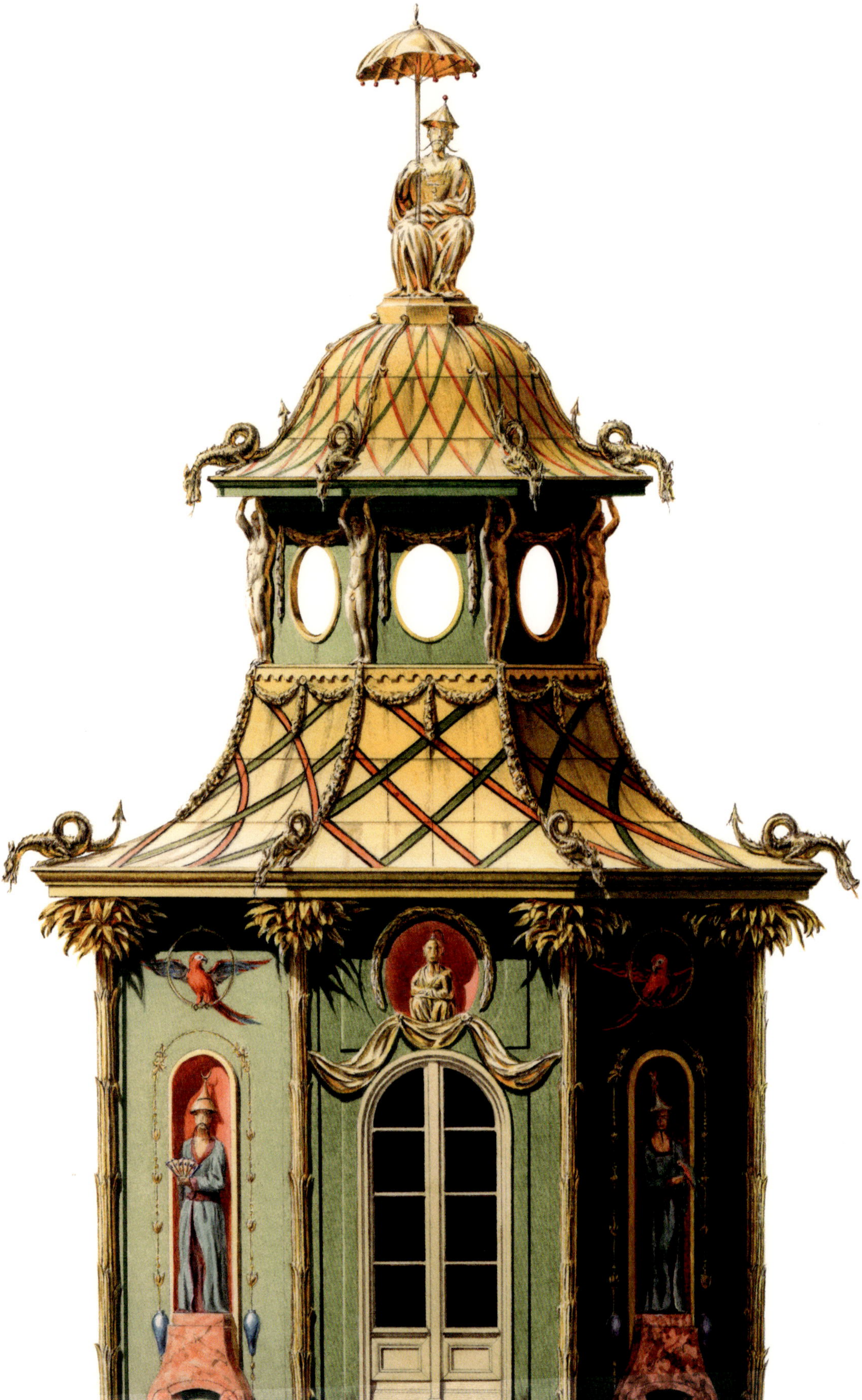

Pagoda at Ménars

Marquis de Marigny, commissioner
Charles De Wailly, architect
built 1772
destroyed

The Marquis de Marigny, brother of Madame de Pompadour, gained his position as Superintendent of Royal Buildings due to her influence. From her he also inherited the Loire Valley estate of Ménars and in 1769, inspired by Sir William Chambers' work at Kew, he invited the foremost architects of his time to design follies and pavilions for the park. Marigny's project is unusual on several levels: first for its avant-garde nature, as it is among the earliest French folly gardens, and also because he resisted the impulse of the picturesque and retained the park's classical lines, which suited the predominantly classical follies he would commission. In 1770, he requested plans for a Chinese kiosk from Jacques-Germain Soufflot, who flatly refused to design in "the Chinese or Arab taste." Marigny took the rebuff in stride and turned to Charles De Wailly.

Presented here is De Wailly's original design, which was slightly modified in execution, though no visual record of the final structure survives. The open rotunda of elongated columns and the Gothic fretwork beneath the curious domed roof lend the base a strongly Venetian character, offset by the miniature pagoda perched atop it, accessed by a spiral stair. The folly is a remarkable composition, an essay in picturesque oppositions that melds wildly disparate architectural styles—Chinese, Gothic and classical—in a structure that itself is a bold juxtaposition between solid and void, massive and delicate, monumental and diminutive.

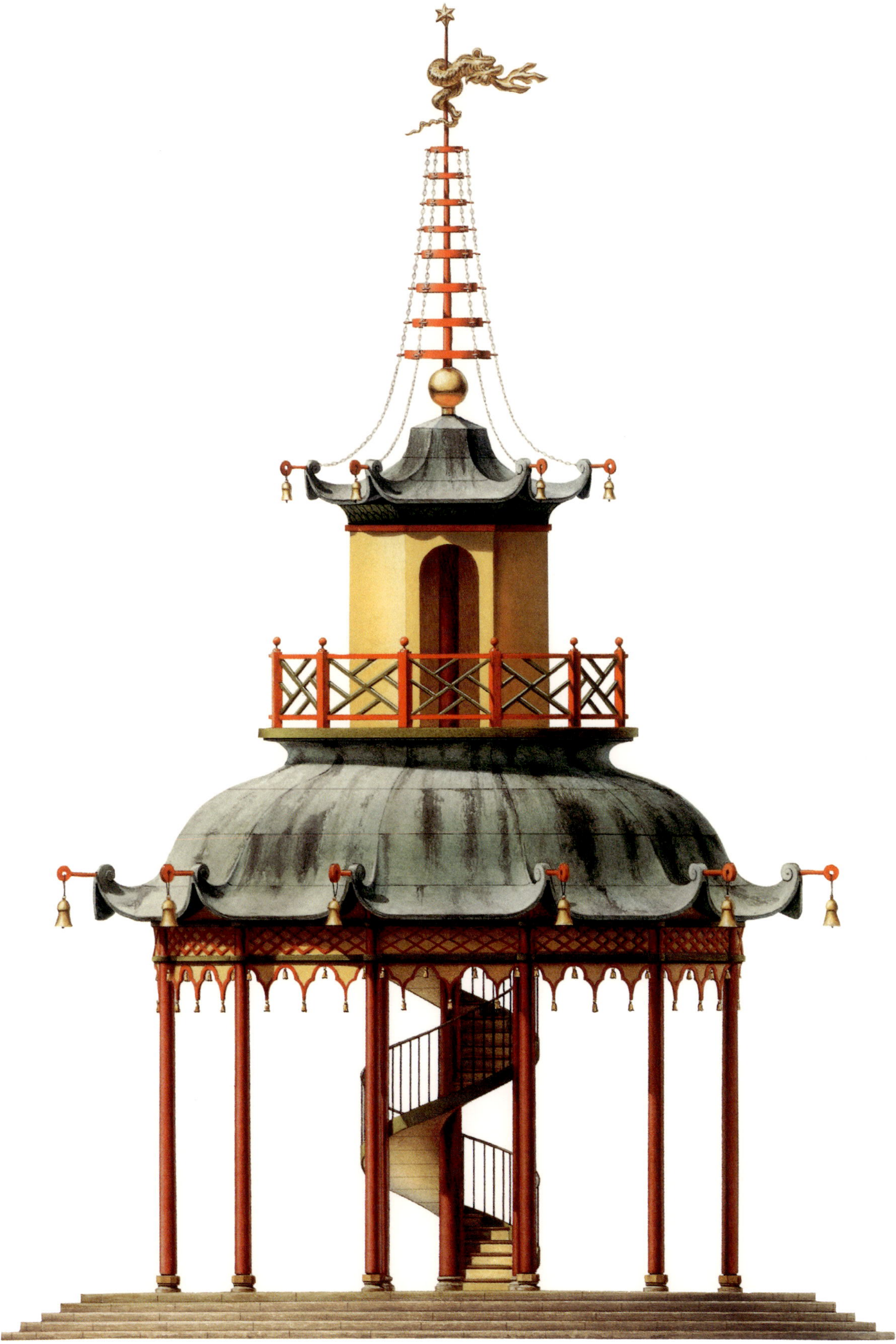

Pavilion of Diana for Trianon Versailles

Marie-Antoinette, commissioner
Antoine Richard, architect
designed 1774
unbuilt project

When Marie-Antoinette decided to transform Louis XV's botanical gardens at Trianon into an English-style landscape garden, she first sought plans from Antoine Richard, who had managed the grounds for more than thirty years. Inevitably his design preserved the majority of the gardens he had earlier created, but the garden was to be crisscrossed by an impenetrable network of paths and watercourses serpenting about twenty-three points of interest—the design recalling the outmoded ornamental gardens of the Régence.

The queen rejected the plan and Richard's revisions, turning for guidance to the Duc d'Harcourt and later still to Hubert Robert and Richard Mique. Eventually Richard's gardens were destroyed and his plans forgotten. Nonetheless this delicate project for a pavilion dedicated to Diana the Huntress—though perhaps not the wisest choice as a cipher for the adolescent queen—is notable for being among the earliest Chinoiserie pavilions designed in France. Its rectilinear plan, palm columns and stolid volumetrics are based on mid-century German precedents and show no influence or knowledge of Sir William Chambers' publications.

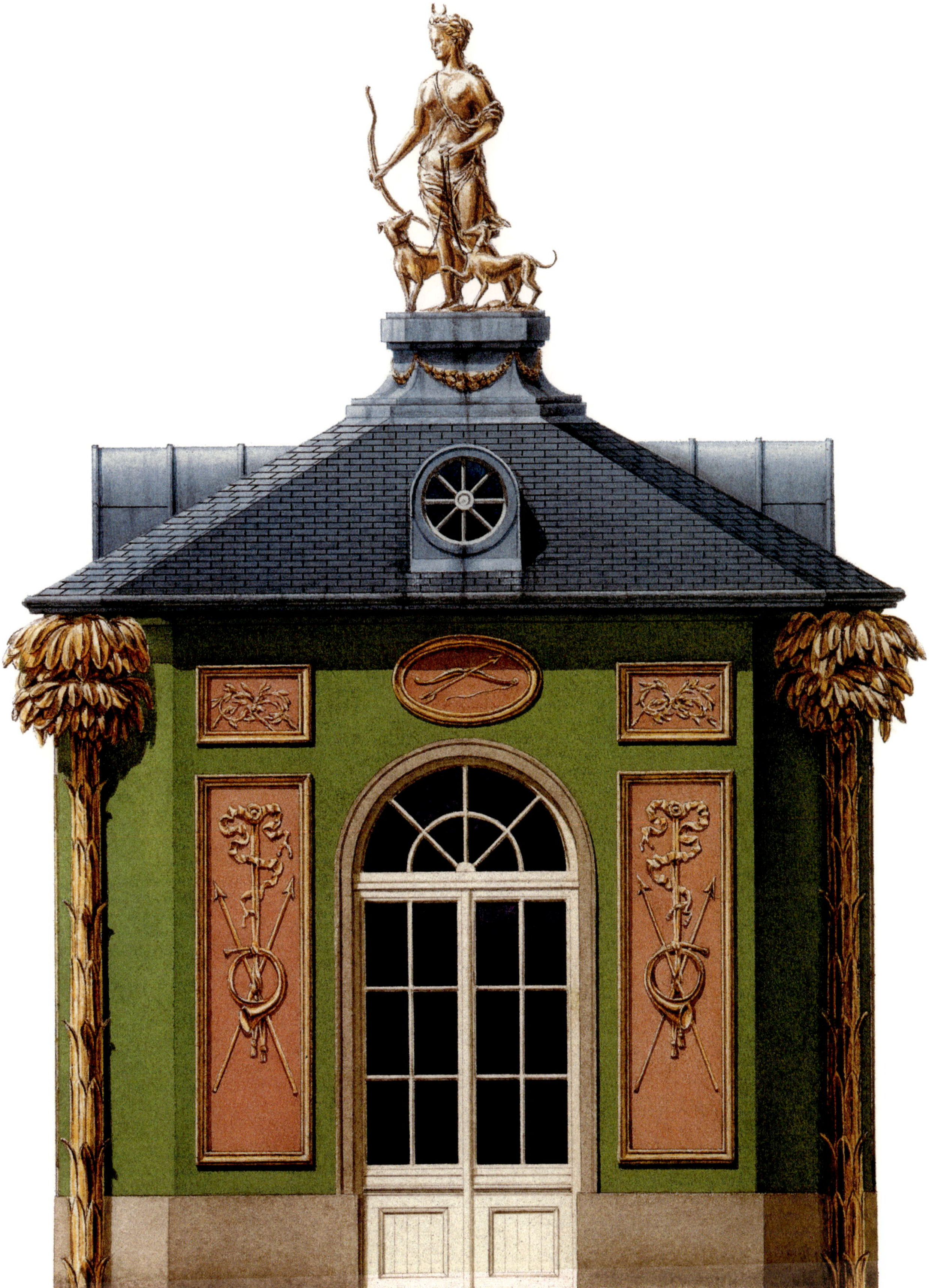

Chinese House for Trianon Versailles

Marie-Antoinette, commissioner
Antoine Richard, architect
designed 1774
unbuilt project

This design for an octagonal pavilion was, with the Pavilion of Diana (*previous page*), the second Chinoiserie folly proposed by Antoine Richard in his plan for the transformations of the botanical gardens at Trianon. Again based on models from the German principalities, the structure has no identifiable Chinese elements; its claim to Chinoiserie rests with its sinuous roofline, palm columns and *craquelure* surface, all drawn from the decorative repertoire of the rococo, which must have appeared outdated to the queen and her entourage, and was subsequently rejected. However, it was exactly this naïve mix of materials, symbols and shapes that characterizes the allure of Chinoiserie in the years before the publication of Sir William Chambers' writings.

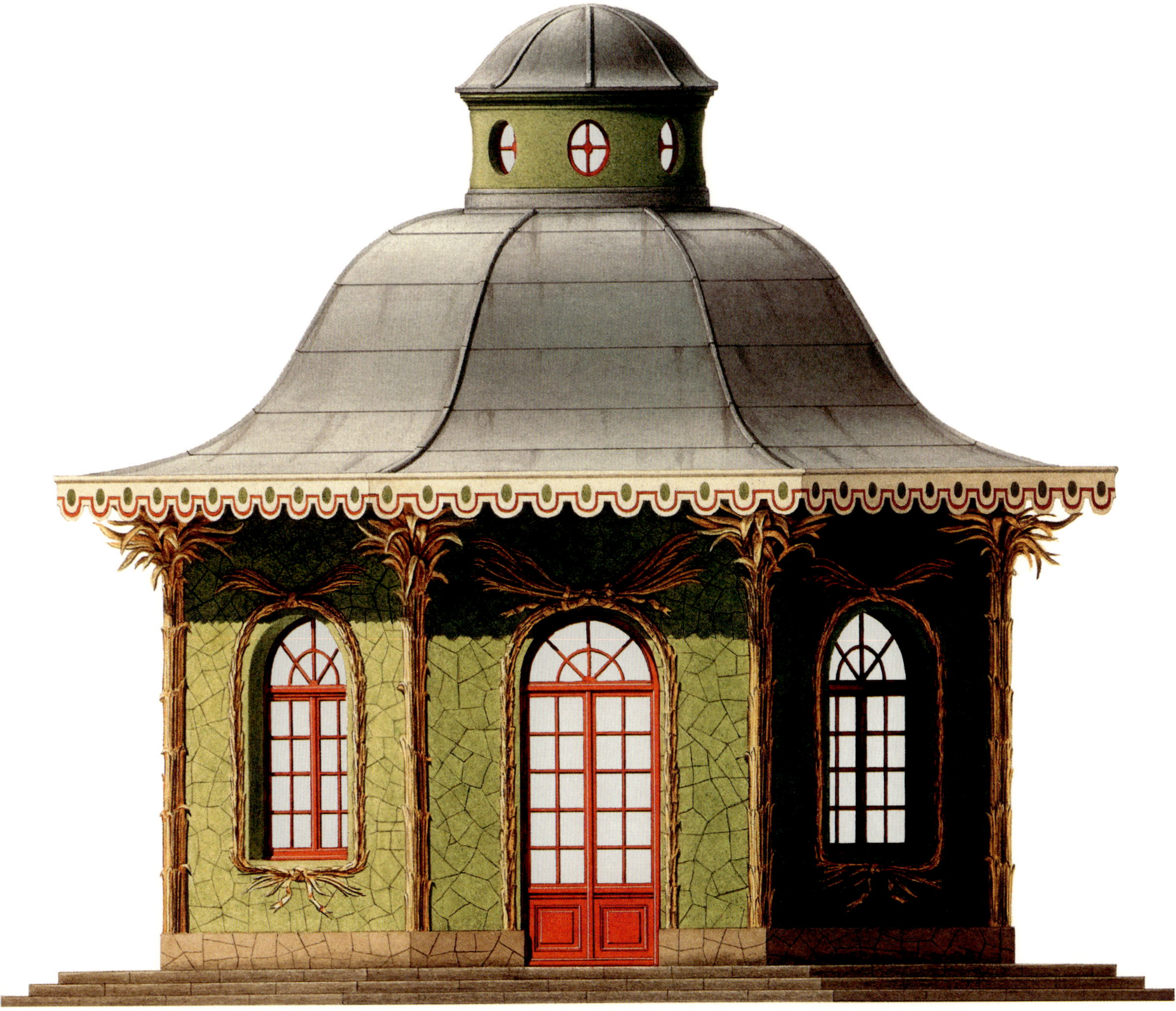

The inhabitants of [China] laugh at the Plantations of our Europeans, which are laid out by the Rule and the Line; because they say anybody may place Trees in equal Rows and uniform Figures.

Joseph Addison

The Chinese Garden *by François Boucher.*

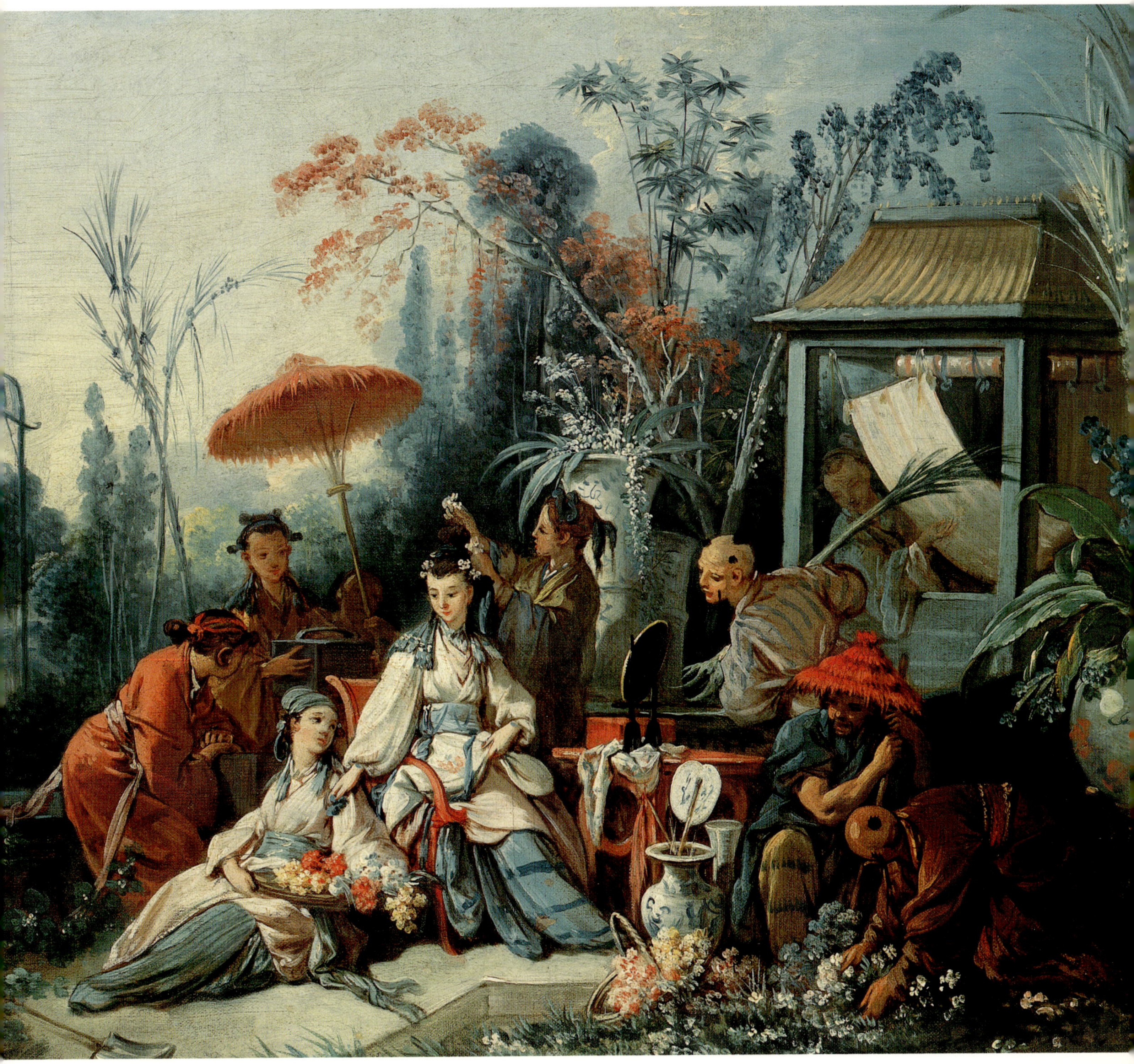

CHINESE RAIN SHELTER FOR TRIANON VERSAILLES

MARIE-ANTOINETTE, COMMISSIONER
ANTOINE RICHARD, ARCHITECT
DESIGNED 1774
UNEXECUTED PROJECT

RICHARD'S SCHEME for Marie-Antoinette's garden at Trianon, though hopelessly old-fashioned, nonetheless was remarkable for the variety of pavilions, kiosks and ornamental structures that anticipated the French mania for garden follies in the last decade before the outbreak of the Revolution. Richard's most picturesque and whimsical structure was this Chinese rain shelter, held up by four simple, painted columns bedecked by flower garlands, and crowned by a domed roof featuring the obligatory array of bells evoking the Orient.

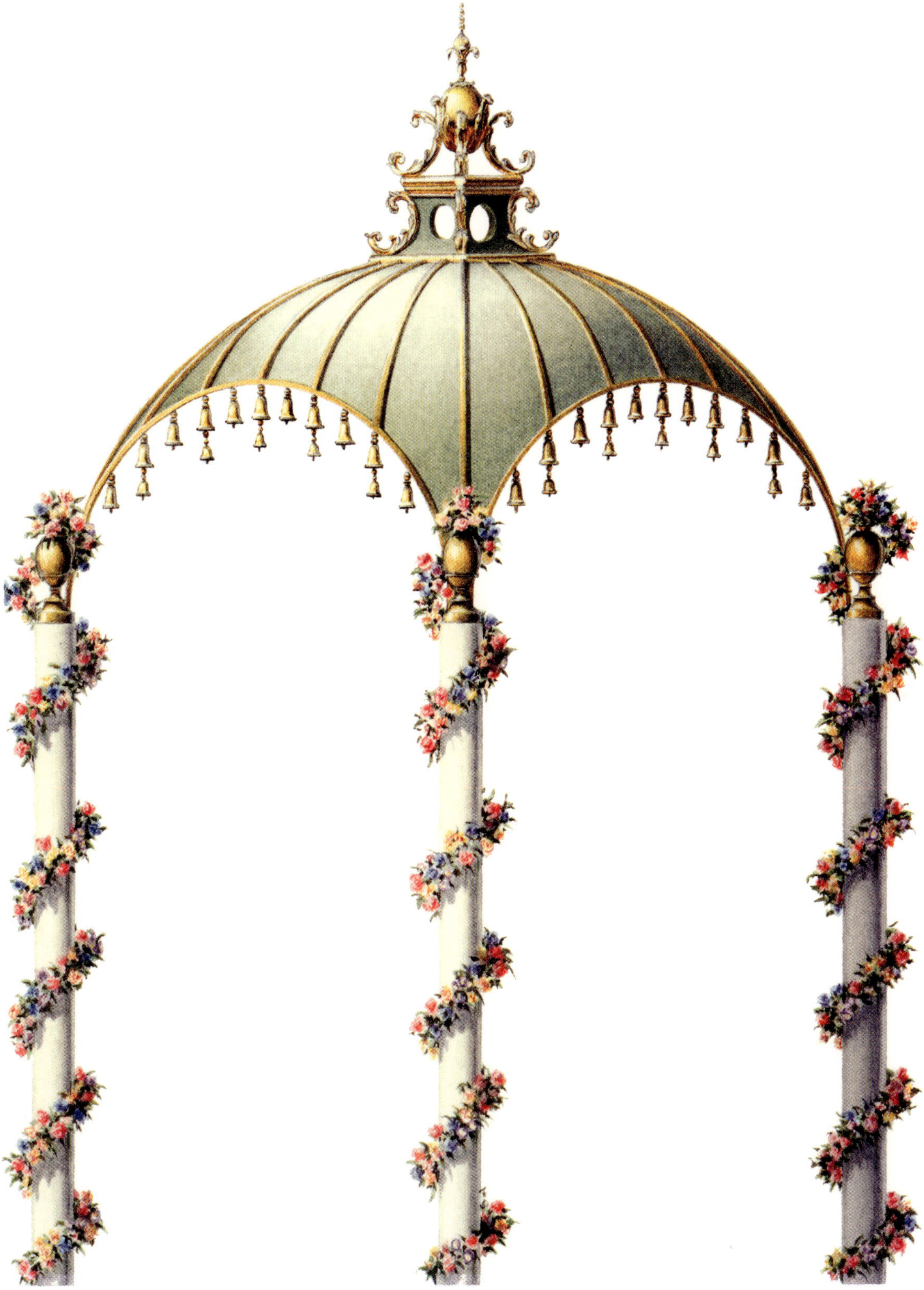

Pagoda at Condé-sur-l'Escault

Prince de Croÿ, commissioner and architect

built circa 1775

destroyed

The Prince de Croÿ, an avid amateur architect who shared his passion for building with Louis XV, designed the pagoda at Condé-sur-l'Escault. Recorded by Georges Le Rouge, who in his haste apparently forgot to mark its position on his engraving of the estate's plan, the pagoda is yet another example of the pervasive influence of Sir William Chambers' publications, as it is virtually identical to a *ting* found in a temple garden in Canton that appeared as plate VI of *The Design of Chinese Buildings*, published in 1757.

Despite its imitative character, the pagoda sports several sculptural details, such as the dolphins riding the roof ends and the pineapple finial—symbol of hospitality and exoticism—that are signature elements of Chinoiserie. Chambers wrote, "A *Ting* is the reception room of a house, the dining hall, or even the courtyard, where the Mandarins hold their meetings. Also, a *Ting* is the main room of a pagoda or a temple."

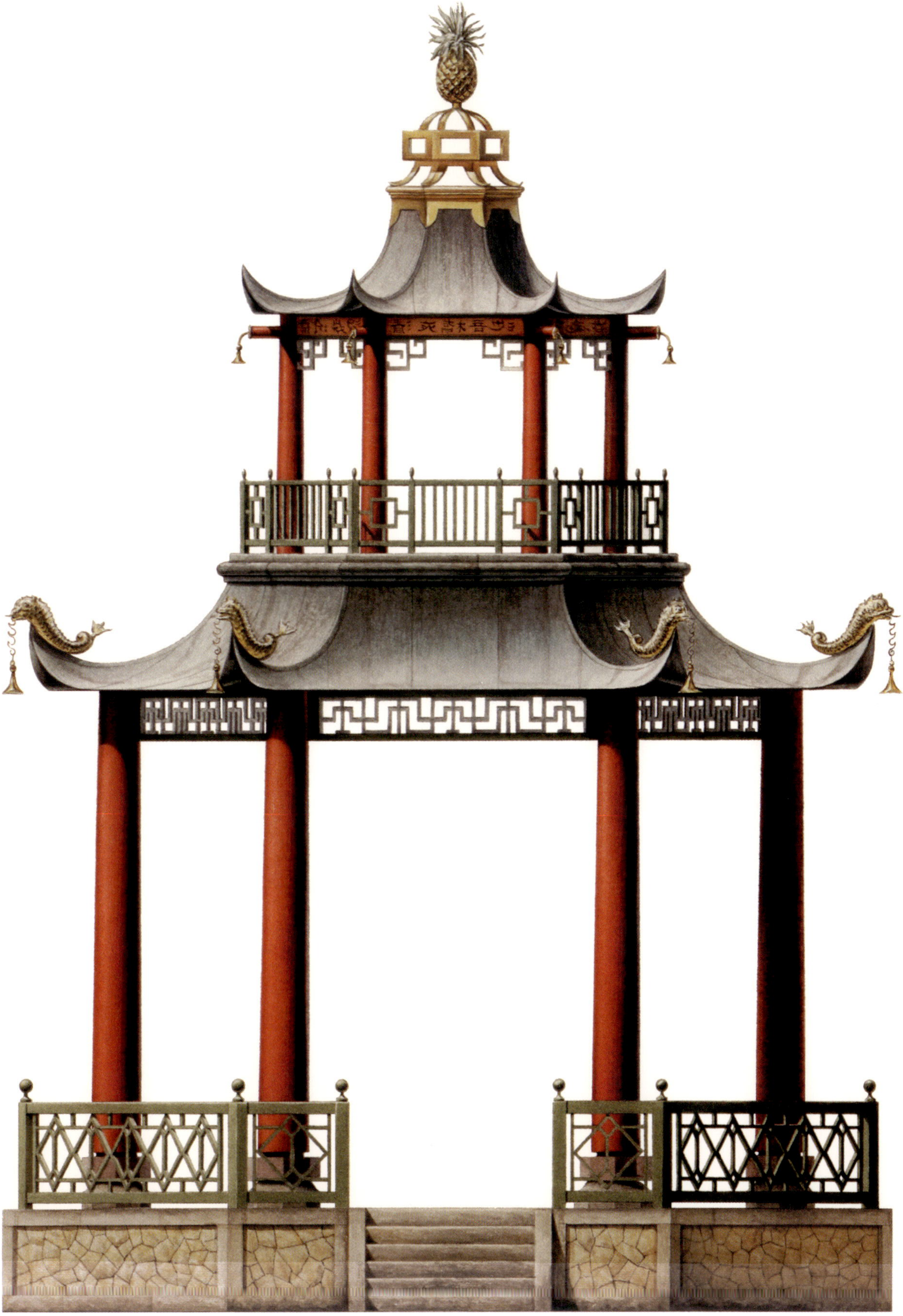

CHINESE PARASOL

UNKNOWN COMMISSIONER
ANONYMOUS ARCHITECT
LATE EIGHTEENTH CENTURY

LIKE THE PALM TREE, often lacquered or gilded, the parasol *à la chinoise* was considered an indispensable accessory in evoking the picturesque and the exotic during the eighteenth century. Though widely employed in the decorative arts and interiors of the French rococo, palms rarely decorated the plethora of French garden follies built late in the century. Though characteristic elements of the so-called "imaginative style" of European Chinoiserie, they would have elicited nothing but befuddlement among the Chinese to whom they were attributed. This design for a small baldachin was doubtless proposed for a retaining wall of the garden of a Parisian *hôtel*, overlooking the street beyond. Entrance porticos in the form of triumphal arches and pagodas perched like miradors lined the walled street frontage of town mansions built along the newly constructed boulevards that ordered the city's expansion in the late 1700s.

The architect, who remains anonymous, noted on the original drawing, "If one would like a larger parasol, one could have four palms instead of two. Instead of wood trussing, the interior of the parasol could be built of iron covered with lead."

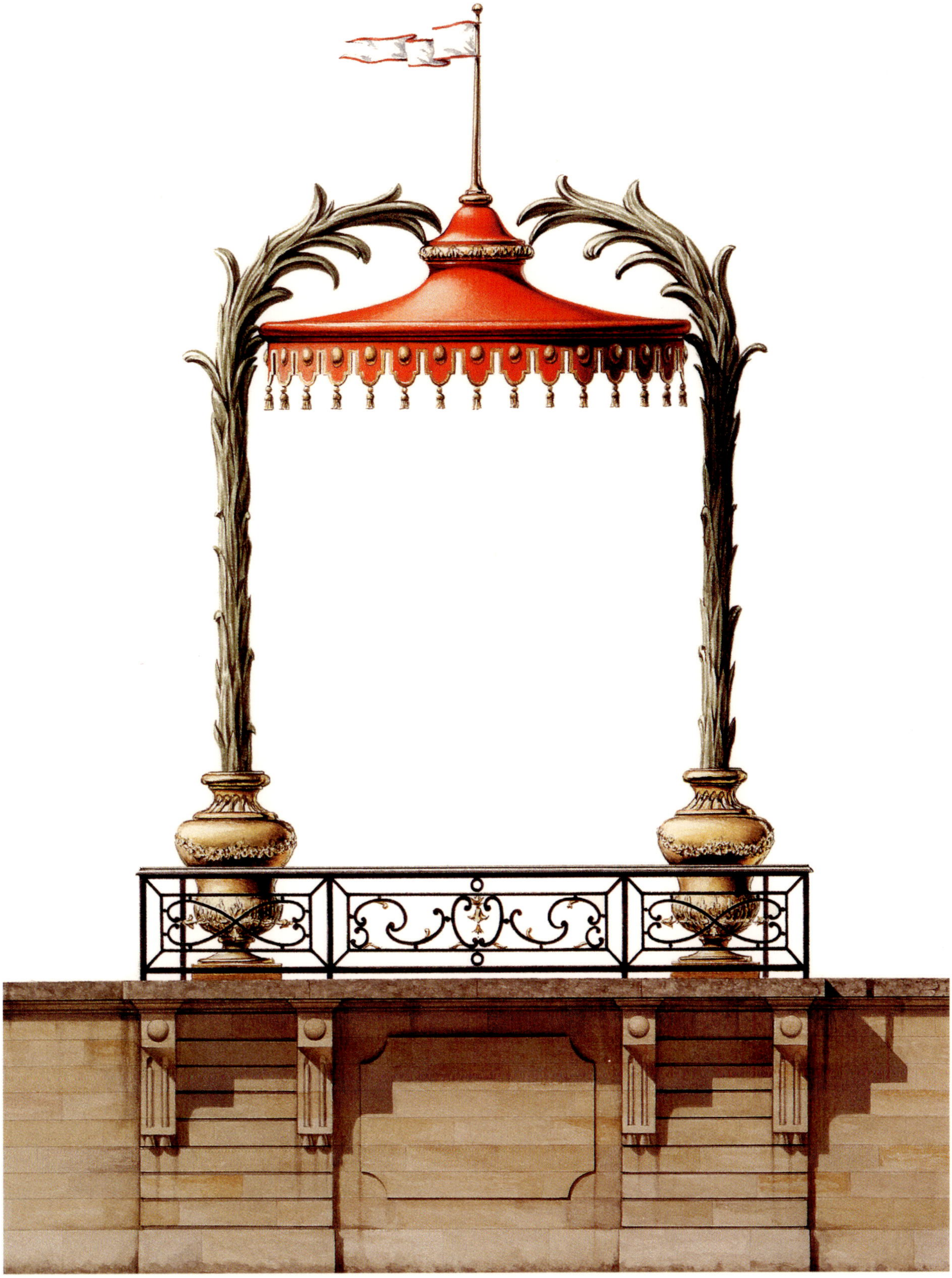

Tartar Tent at Parc Monceau

Duc de Chartres, commissioner
Louis Carrogis, alias Carmontelle, architect
built circa 1775
destroyed

The parc monceau, Paris, was created by Louis Carrogis, known as Carmontelle, for the Duc de Chartres. Carmontelle was a dedicated maximalist with more fantasy and enthusiasm than taste, and the resulting garden met a cold reception. Carmontelle justified his work by writing, "If one can transform a picturesque garden into a land of illusions, why not do so, since only illusions amuse…we should bring the changing scenes of opera into our gardens, letting us see, in reality, what the most accomplished painters offer on canvas—all periods and places."

The Tartar Tent was exactly one of these stage sets, an addition to the main pavilion disguised with painted metal sheets and strategically placed plantings to appear to be a detached garden tent. Unusual in that it was among the first of its kind constructed in durable materials and not fabric, the tent doubtless inspired François Racine de Monville to erect his own Siamese Tent at the Désert de Retz (*p. 79*).

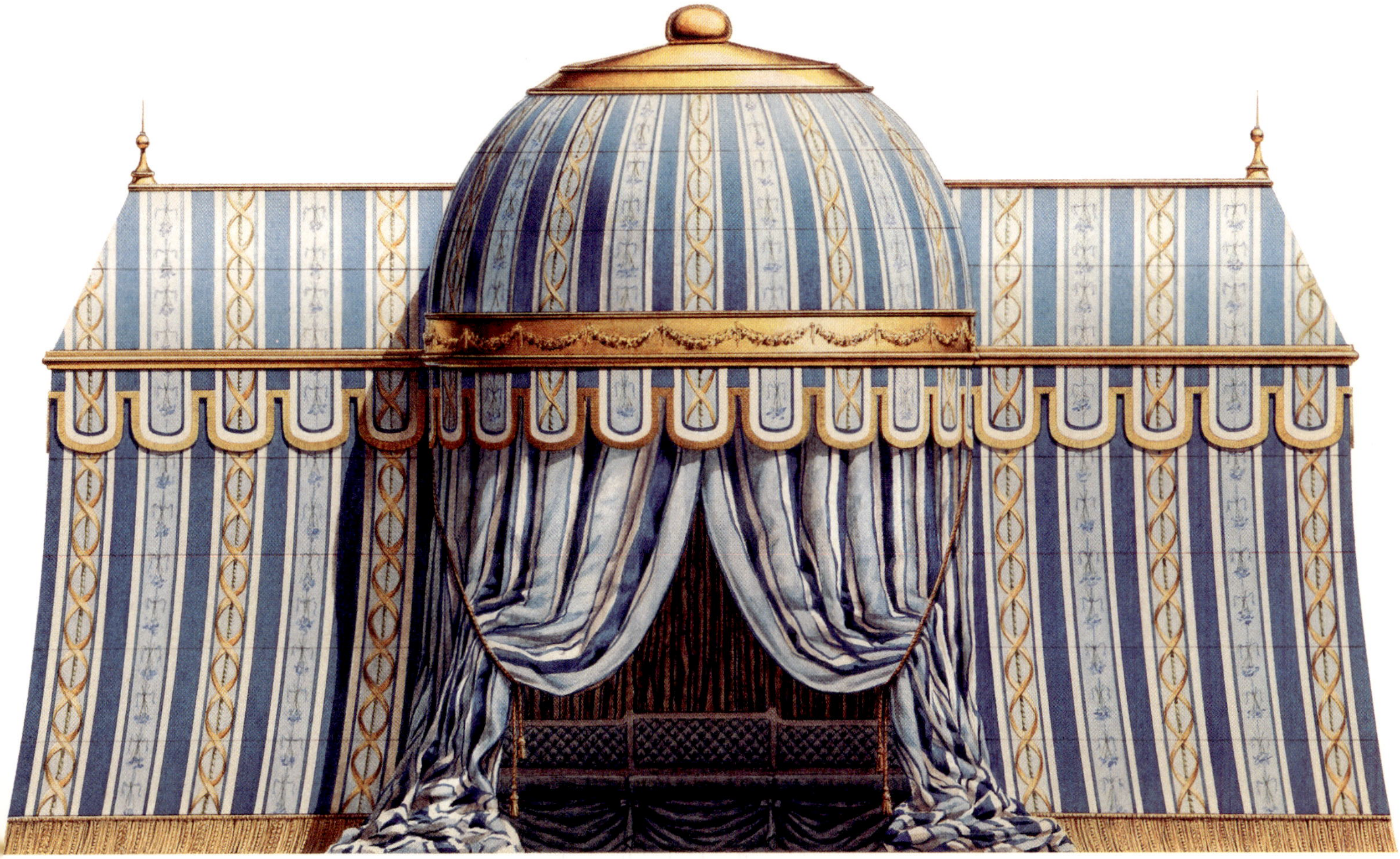

Tent at Parc Monceau

Duc de Chartres, commissioner
Louis Carrogis, alias Carmontelle, architect
built circa 1775
destroyed

Carmontelle, at heart a man of the theater, wrote of his work at Parc Monceau, "It was certainly not an English garden that one wanted to make at Monceau but precisely what is being said when criticizing it: to unite all times and all places in a single garden. It is a simple fantasy, the desire to have an extraordinary garden, a pure amusement, and not the desire to imitate a nation [England] that, in creating natural gardens, rolls its lawns and spoils nature by everywhere exhibiting the circumscribed art of the unimaginative gardener." Certainly nothing in the design of Parc Monceau would ever be mistaken for an English landscape park, and if anything it more closely resembled a modern amusement park, with several dozen attractions scattered across the landscape and appropriately costumed servants attending each folly, including turbaned servants offering camel rides.

In an engraved view drawn and published by Carmontelle himself, the camel waited near this charming, fabric-draped tent. A large, exedra-shaped bench stood nearby, also artfully draped, the ensemble and the elaborately clothed and bewigged visitors creating a tableau redolent of the atmosphere of slightly absurd refinement that permeated the French Anglo-Chinese folly garden.

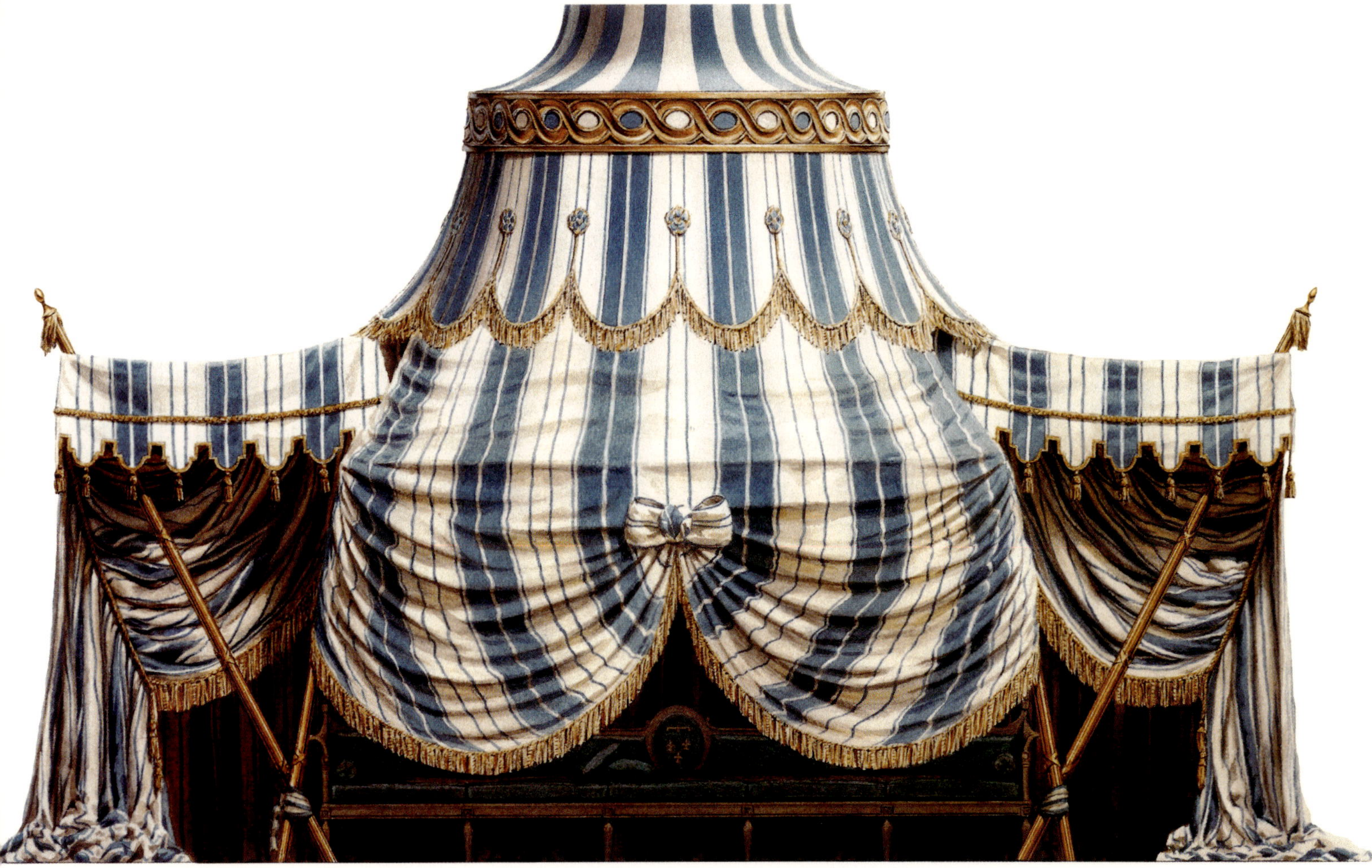

"A Graceful Disorder"

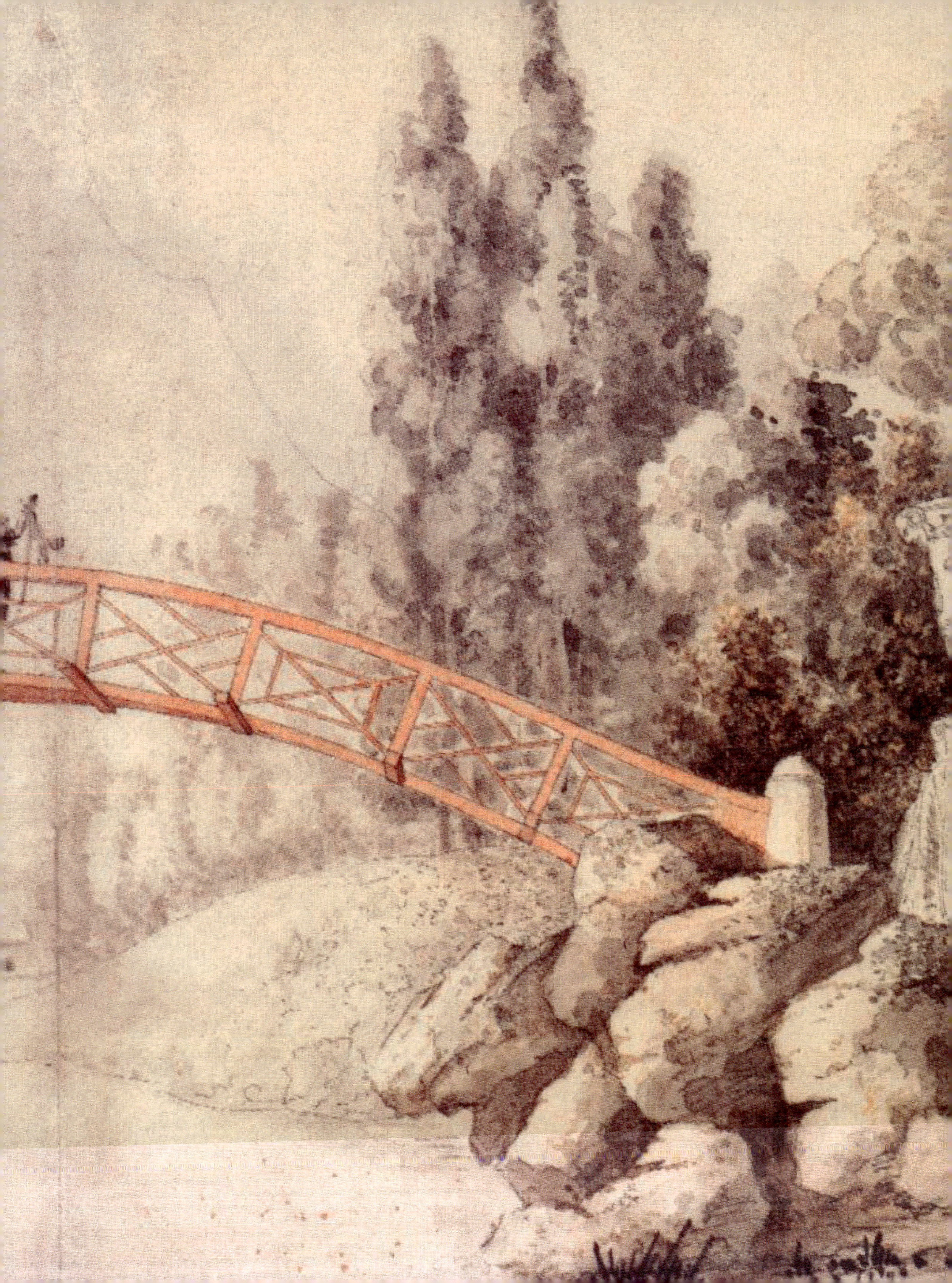

Previous pages: a watercolor of the Chinese bridge at Bagatelle drawn by François-Joseph Bélanger, its architect.

"A Graceful Disorder"

IF CYRIL CONNOLLY defined garden pavilions as "exercises in simplicity," Chinoiserie pagodas can be described as exercises in eccentricity. The embodiment of the picturesque, these small buildings were symbols of a better world, the architectural antithesis of absolutism, and it is little wonder they sprang up so vigorously in the waning decades of the ancien régime.

Gardens and their ornaments have always been considered a reflection of the existing political order or a projection of a utopian society, and the *jardin à la française,* following the model of Versailles, was the horticultural mirror of royal authority. As late as 1750 the abbé Pluche compared the work of the garden designer to that of a legislator, who took it upon himself to uproot barbarism and implant civilization among the people, but it was exactly this asphyxiating degree of civilization that detractors saw as the enemy of openness and enlightenment. Voltaire noted that an English oak—a symbol of freedom—would surely die if transplanted to the clipped world of Marly. "Almost nothing regular, thank God," he remarked of his own garden at Ferney.

A generation before the French Revolution, the English garden, and by extension the *jardin anglo-chinois,* its Continental offspring, had become the mirrors of princes and, despite their illusionistic displays, emblems of a new order. "Imagination is the natural ally of freedom," wrote the abbé Jacques de Lille at the end of the ancien régime, and his book-length poem, *Les Jardins,* eulogized the great gardens of Le Nôtre and Louis XIV as the retreats of ancient heroes and Olympian gods. "Kings are condemned to magnificence," he wrote; "every bosquet is a temple, every marble a deity." Versailles and Marly, imbued with a pompous grandeur that soon fatigued, are evoked in counterpoint to the brimming vitality of the new Anglo-Chinese landscape garden, whose picturesque scenes of studied

Chinoiseries

disorder and foreign novelty were where the cleric's sensibilities truly resided, in gardens imagining Cathay.

The ostensible frivolity of Chinoiserie follies, frankly designed and more often resembling overscaled toys than actual buildings, nonetheless revealed a deep, unspoken sentiment: their authenticity was validated by the longings of those who had built them. Certain Western theorists understood Chinese landscape design; William Temple, Jean-Denis Attiret and Sir William Chambers, each a generation apart, articulated both its motivating principles and underlying logic. These ideas were taken up and debated by other writers, many of whom created their own gardens, and entered the general theory of the art of gardening by the mid-eighteenth century. But clearly certain fundamental ideas were in fundamental opposition: architectural creations in China were considered an element of the landscape; in Europe, architecture dominated and ordered the landscape.

Outward appearances notwithstanding, the pictorial impulse of the landscape garden did nothing to change the established European dynamic between nature and architecture: the irregular simply replaced the symmetrical, and these new gardens were conceived as a highly decorative stage upon which to pursue political and philosophical questions as well as childish pastimes. All that was required was picturesque beauty and a sense of the exotic that could be easily translated into architecture *à la chinoise*.

In execution, Chinoiserie rarely if ever rose above decoration: its underlying attraction—the call of another, richer world—was subsumed in frivolity, and the style was employed indiscriminately to add pictorial charm to a landscape. While foreign forms were often employed, architects and builders, ignorant of

"A Graceful Disorder"

A perspective view of the Porcelain Trianon (p. 31); Versailles is seen in the distance.

CHINOISERIES

"A Graceful Disorder"

the rules that underpinned them, could happily indulge in picturesque pastiche, and so Chinoiserie came to be defined by the unexpected, the grotesque and the bizarre—an outgrowth of the light-hearted theatricality of the rococo, itself a reaction to the decorous rigidity of the Age of Louis XIV.

The Sun King's Porcelain Trianon (*pp. 31, 59*) stood sixteen years but acquired near-mythic fame through numerous engravings and descriptions circulating among the major courts of Europe. Its exoticism sprang from association and opulence—its Baroque decoration was imbued with the Orient by projected meaning, since one only sees what one knows, and one knew virtually nothing of Chinese architecture—and in that sense it was a quintessential Chinoiserie structure. Underscoring the compound's unique precedence, almost fifty years would pass before its first offspring appeared, curiously not in France but Bavaria. The Elector Max Emmanuel had spent several years in exile at Versailles during the War of the Spanish Succession, and the Pagodenburg, finished in 1719 in the park of Nymphenburg near Munich, was his own free interpretation of the Porcelain Trianon, a classical pavilion with Chinoiserie interiors.

Much grander in scope was Schloss Pilnitz near Dresden, built for August the Strong by Matthaeus Daniel Pöppelmann; the first phase of the Baroque residence was nearing completion when Fischer von Erlach published his *Entwurf einer historischen Architektur* in 1721 and Pöppelmann designed the main body of the Schloss with sloped roofs and deep coves animated by silhouettes of Chinese

*Opposite: the Indian House at Brühl, completed 1753, also called "la Maison sans gêne."
Painting attributed to Franz Jacob Rousseau.*

Chinoiseries

characters—the coves an enduring detail, completely foreign to Chinese architecture, that would become characteristic of German Chinoiserie and still recur at the Japanese House at Paretz (*p. 151*) at century's end.

The first true Chinoiserie folly was the Trèfle, or Cloverleaf, built by the French architect Emmanuel Héré between 1738 and 1741 at Lunéville, the provincial Lorraine court of the exiled Polish king, Stanislas Leszczynski. A masonry pavilion with a tri-lobed plan, the Trèfle also featured a flat-pitched, undulating roof surmounted by a latticed clerestory drum, itself crowned by a flaring conical roof. The Trèfle was but one of several exotic pavilions erected in Lunéville's park, which the king furnished as if it were an enormous, open-air *Wunderkammer,* and Frederick the Great would use it as the model for his own Chinese House at Sans Souci, built in 1755 after engravings furnished by Héré.

Frederick's sister, Queen Ulrike of Sweden, followed her brother's example: in 1753 a prefabricated Chinese House designed by Nicodemus Tessin, featuring corner palm columns and undulating roofs, was secretly erected at Drottningholm as a surprise birthday gift, its presentation celebrated with an elaborate Chinese fête. When it fell to disrepair, the pavilion was replaced by a permanent residence in 1763, described by the Englishman Nathaniel Wraxall in 1775:

> *In the gardens the Queen Dowager has lately built a little palace of pleasure, in a semi-circular form, composed of several apartments fitted up in that taste*

Opposite: The Chinese pavilion at Bailystok, engraved by Michael Heindrich Rentz after Johann Klemm.

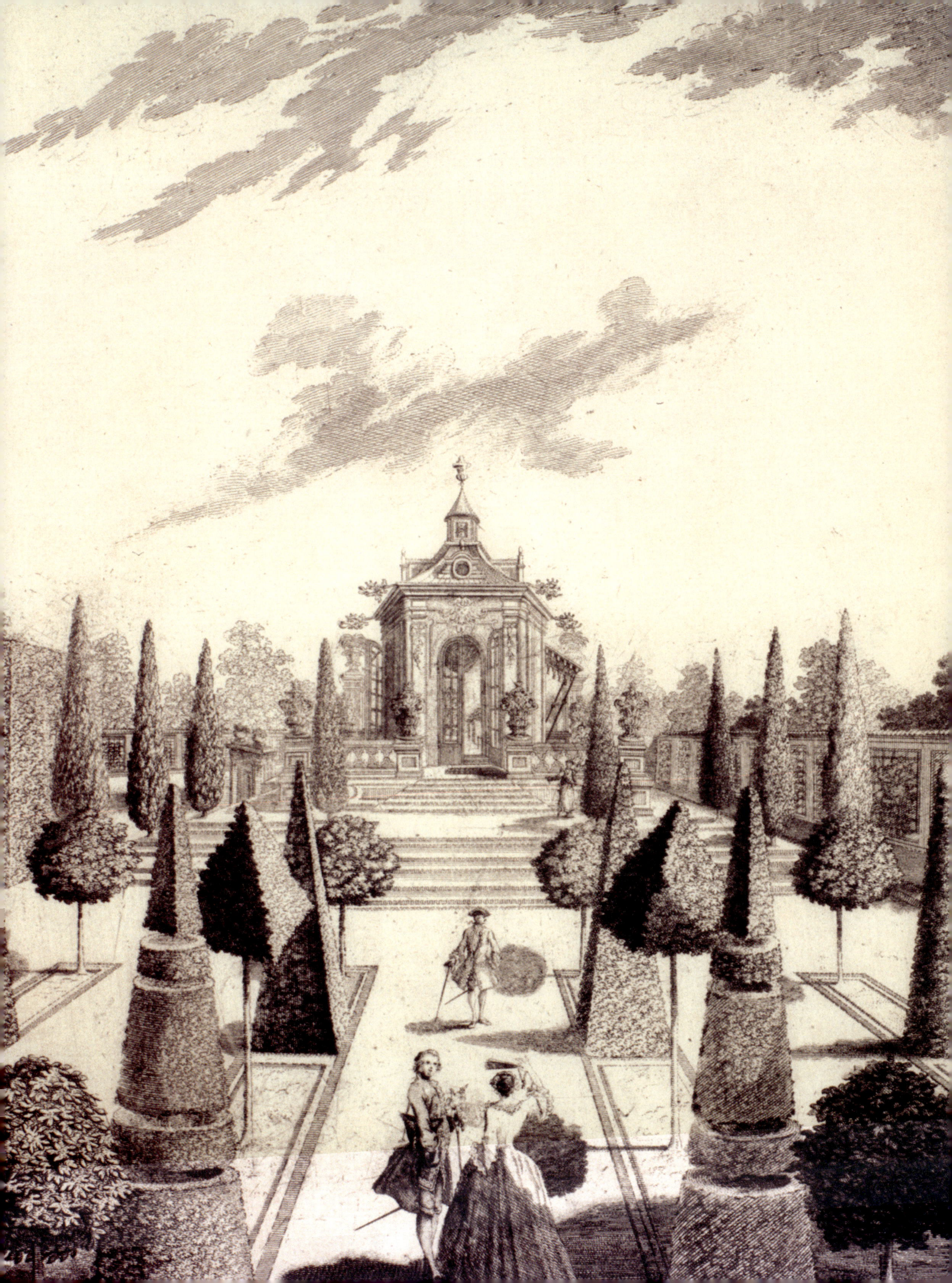

Chinoiseries

"A Graceful Disorder"

which we usually call Chinese; though, unless a few mandarins and vases of China form this style, of which we really know scarcely anything, it may just as well be called a European structure, where whimsy and caprice form the predominant character and spread a grotesque air through the whole.

While the earliest Chinoiserie-inspired buildings erected at Nymphenburg and elsewhere had little in their outward appearance to distinguish them, the Chinoiserie pavilions to follow, at Bruchsaal, Karlsruhe and Veithöchheim, became increasingly theatrical manifestations of rococo fantasy, as German architects employed a characteristic repertoire of winsome ornament—including palm trees, mandarins, dragons, pineapples and bells—to suggest a completely imaginary Orient. Tellingly, contemporaries named the Indian House at Brühl (*p. 61*), completed in 1753, *la Maison sans gêne*, its exoticism expressed by bright pink façades, exuberant decorative details and a dragon-bedecked roof.

A great variety of Chinoiserie flourished in the German states in the 1750s, a period of relative political calm. Most courts employed highly capable architects and decorators, and even small principalities nurtured such talents as Paul Egell, who designed the Chinoise at Oggersheim (*p. 33*), one of the most beautiful and evocative examples of rococo Chinoiserie. The Seven Years' War abruptly halted such frivolous constructions and in the ensuing peace Sir William Chambers captured the attention of Continental gardeners, bringing the colorful, bizarre reign of German Chinoiserie to a close.

*O*pposite: the Chinese House at Steinhöffel by Friedrich Gilly, its architect. *Gilly would reprise this design for the Japanese House at Paretz (p. 151).*

Chinoiseries

The first English pagodas—diminutive, four-square summerhouses built of open fretwork—appeared in the late 1730s, with the most prominent early example, the House of Confucius, built at Kew after plans by Joseph Goupy in 1745. An extensive China trade through the East India Company had established a strong English appetite for Chinese imports, and the nobility assimilated Eastern porcelain, lacquerware and carpets so completely into their interiors that, like tea itself, they became thoroughly English commodities by the mid-eighteenth century.

Apparently, the initial impulse sparking the phenomenon was nothing more compelling than the sentimental wish to build a souvenir of China in a corner of an aristocratic park. Conditioned by the fashion for erecting antique temples on their estates, the English nobility took to the fad with relish and by mid-century William Halfpenny (alias Michael Hoare) began to publish a series of *New Designs for Chinese Temples,* his title confirming the English pagoda's classical progenitors.

In contrast to the masonry walls and solid volumetrics that characterized German pavilions, English pagodas were mostly insubstantial stick-and-lathe structures encrusted with rococo scrollwork, their ornaments a pastiche of Gothic elements, classically derived swags and grotesques, and naïve symbols of the Orient—men with coolie hats and Confucian moustaches, devil-tongued dragons and a plethora of bells. The English style evolved from imported Chinese lacquerwork and furniture, whose decorative fretwork patterns were taken up by influential furniture makers such as Thomas Chippendale and blended with the Strawberry Hill Gothic then also in vogue.

Opposite: A Chinoiserie cartouche by Gabriel Huquier the Elder.

"A Graceful Disorder"

Chinoiseries

England's rage for pagodas was an intense but brief efflorescence, spanning a little over a decade's time. Like every fad, novelty and outlandishness incited its rapid spread and in due time surfeit and excess ensured its abrupt demise. Fashion had turned, with aristocratic patrons freshly wary of indiscriminate ornament: Horace Walpole, acid-tongued barometer of taste, dismissed Chinoiseries as "paltry" in 1753, after lauding their whimsy and originality but three years earlier.

Appropriated by the Chinese from nomadic tents, the concave, upturned roof—the most superficial but emblematic of adaptations—became Chinoiserie's most evocative element and a stock component of the repertoire of rococo architecture. Often adorned with dragons, bells, spheres, *chattras* or all of the above, the characteristic peak dominated countless bosquets and shimmered through the verdure of hundreds of gardens from Sweden to Sicily, with the most outlandish designs found in France, Russia and the parks of Germany's numerous princely states.

Usually built of wood, painted board and sheet metal, pagodas embodied the transience of their nomadic ancestors, and it was exactly their fugitive nature that elicited enchantment and led them almost invariably to be set beside, or even in, the mercurial element of water. As if to ground their floating image, pagodas were often built on rockwork bases—torturously worked grottoes and diminutive mountains gushing miniature cascades that evoked Chinese landscapes. Petromania, the love of bizarrely formed rocks, was an ancient Chinese tradition that reached its apogee in the tenth century under the reign of Emperor Huizong, who ennobled the most beautiful rock in his vast collection.

Sir William Chambers noted that the Chinese were unsurpassed in composing artificial rockworks, and promoted their picturesque uses in *The Design of*

"A Graceful Disorder"

Chinese Buildings (1757). A section of the book offered a literal how-to manual for folly builders, advising, for example, that rugged, irregular steps should lead to the little buildings perched atop them.

As ephemeral as Chinoiserie structures appeared, expense was rarely an object; the France of Louis XVI was littered with ministers, financiers and aristocrats ruined by their Anglo-Chinese gardens: the Duc de Choiseul at Chanteloup (*pp. 83, 130-131*) and the Baron de Sainte-James at his Folie in Neuilly (*pp. 139, 141*) are but two prominent examples, and her architectural extravagances at Trianon (*pp. 39, 41, 45, 71, 73, 127*) would be among the most damning accusations raised against Marie-Antoinette during the Revolution. Even Russia's Catherine II, reminded of the exorbitant cost of her Chinese village at Tsarskoje Selo, shrugged and replied, "So be it, it is my caprice."

 The Prince de Ligne was a typical debt-ridden folly builder, whose wife secretly wrote to the superintendent of his estates, begging to divert her husband from building any more pagodas or surely they would end bankrupt. Those follies already built had cost fortunes and her husband rarely visited Baudour, what further need did they have of pagodas, facing ruin? She closed by instructing the superintendent to burn her letter, preserved today in the archives of Beloeil. The German garden theorist Christian Hirschfeld had already noted this French proclivity years before the Princesse de Ligne's distress, writing in 1779, "In England people work more for themselves. In France it is not so much with the aim of pleasing the eye, or meeting the demands of convenience, that the work is done, but to satisfy the cravings of vanity, which often swallows up an entire fortune."

Carrousel at Trianon
Versailles

Marie-Antoinette, commissioner
Richard Mique, architect
built 1776
destroyed

In a pointed mark of fidelity, Louis XVI gave the Trianon, imprinted with the memory of his predecessors' mistresses, to his young queen upon ascending to the throne in 1774. Marie-Antoinette, a sheltered adolescent intimidated by the French court, quickly sought refuge there, creating a fiercely private domain where even her husband was required to ask permission to visit. The Carrousel was her first building project, designed by her personal architect, Richard Mique, in 1776. A demi-lune Chinoiserie arcade bracketed the structure, providing shade for spectators. Erected just to the west of the Petit Trianon, the Carrousel was inspired by a similar *jeu de bague* built by the Duc de Chartres at Parc Monceau and captures the longing for fantasy and innocent amusements which would characterize the queen's undertakings at Trianon.

Two servants in a subterranean tunnel rotated the Carrousel as ladies sat on the painted peacock seats and gentlemen on the gilded dragons, straining in turn for the gold ring dangling barely within reach with short batons. Though a perfect bit of scenography, the Carrousel was not without its faults: dozens of tiny bells originally ringed the roofline, but they drove the queen to distraction and were ordered removed. Likewise, the extravagant sculpted animal seats, apparently as uncomfortable as they were picturesque, were replaced with plain wooden seats soon after the Carrousel's completion.

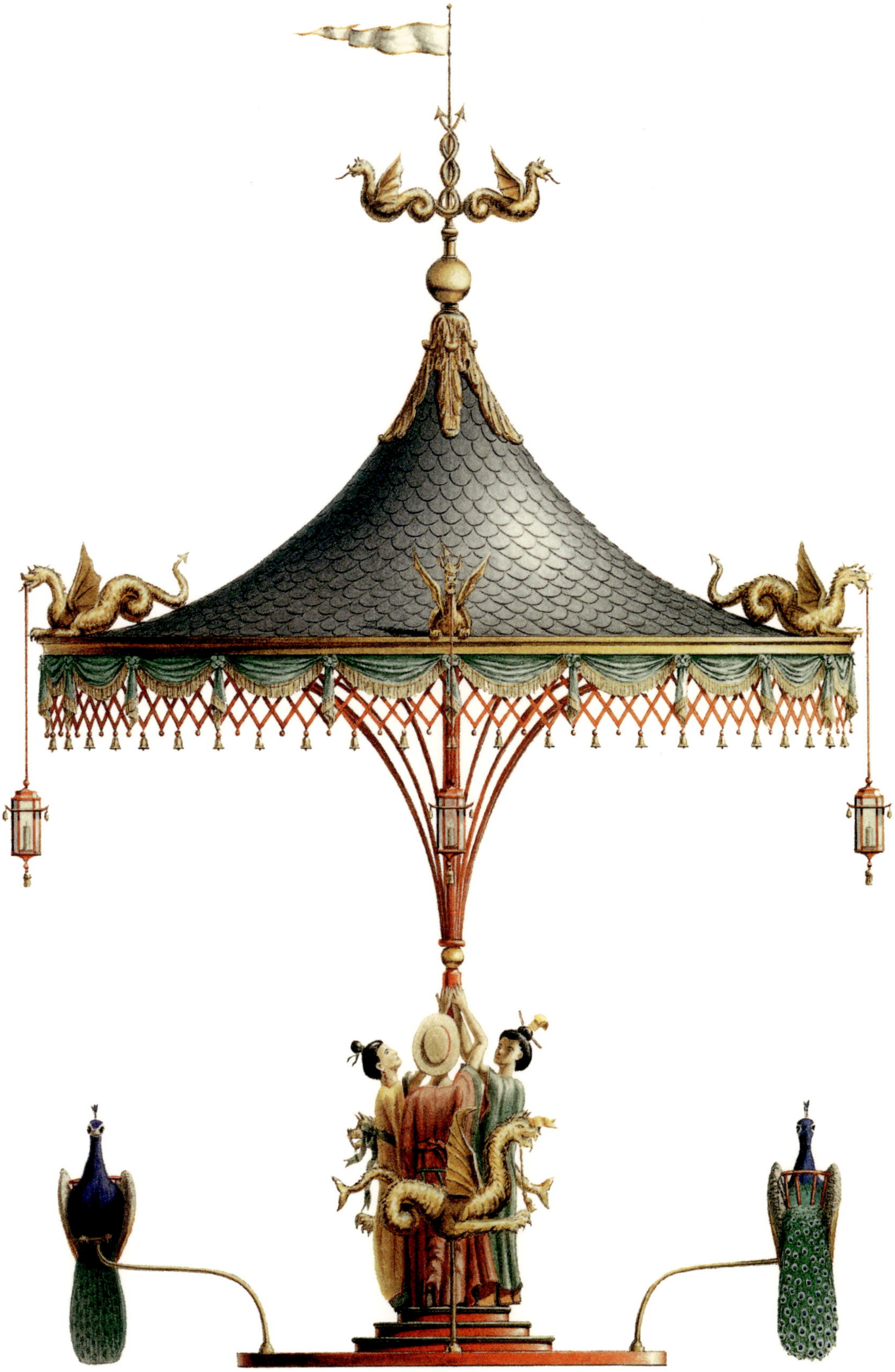

Pagoda for Trianon Versailles

Marie-Antoinette, commissioner
Richard Mique, architect
designed 1777
unbuilt project

RICHARD MIQUE'S unrealized project for a pagoda was designed for Marie-Antoinette's *anglo-chinois* gardens at Trianon. Typical of Germanic Chinoiserie pavilions, it illustrates the fact that its architect was trained at the court of King Stanislas Leszczynski at Lunéville. There, the architect Emmanuel Héré and the king had created an exuberant, eclectic style which reflected the king's long, peripatetic exile across Europe and the German principalities.

Stanislas' small court became an important cultural center, and the gardens at Lunéville were a rococo wonderland, unabashedly mixing periods and styles, and using the whole of Europe, as well as Turkey and China, as sources of inspiration. Mique's artistic sensibilities were profoundly influenced by this milieu; he became the protégé of Queen Marie Leszczynska soon after his arrival in Versailles, and when requested to design for Marie-Antoinette he did not hesitate to employ the aesthetic vocabulary he learned at Lunéville—indeed his sole point of reference for such an undertaking—to propose a pagoda for Trianon.

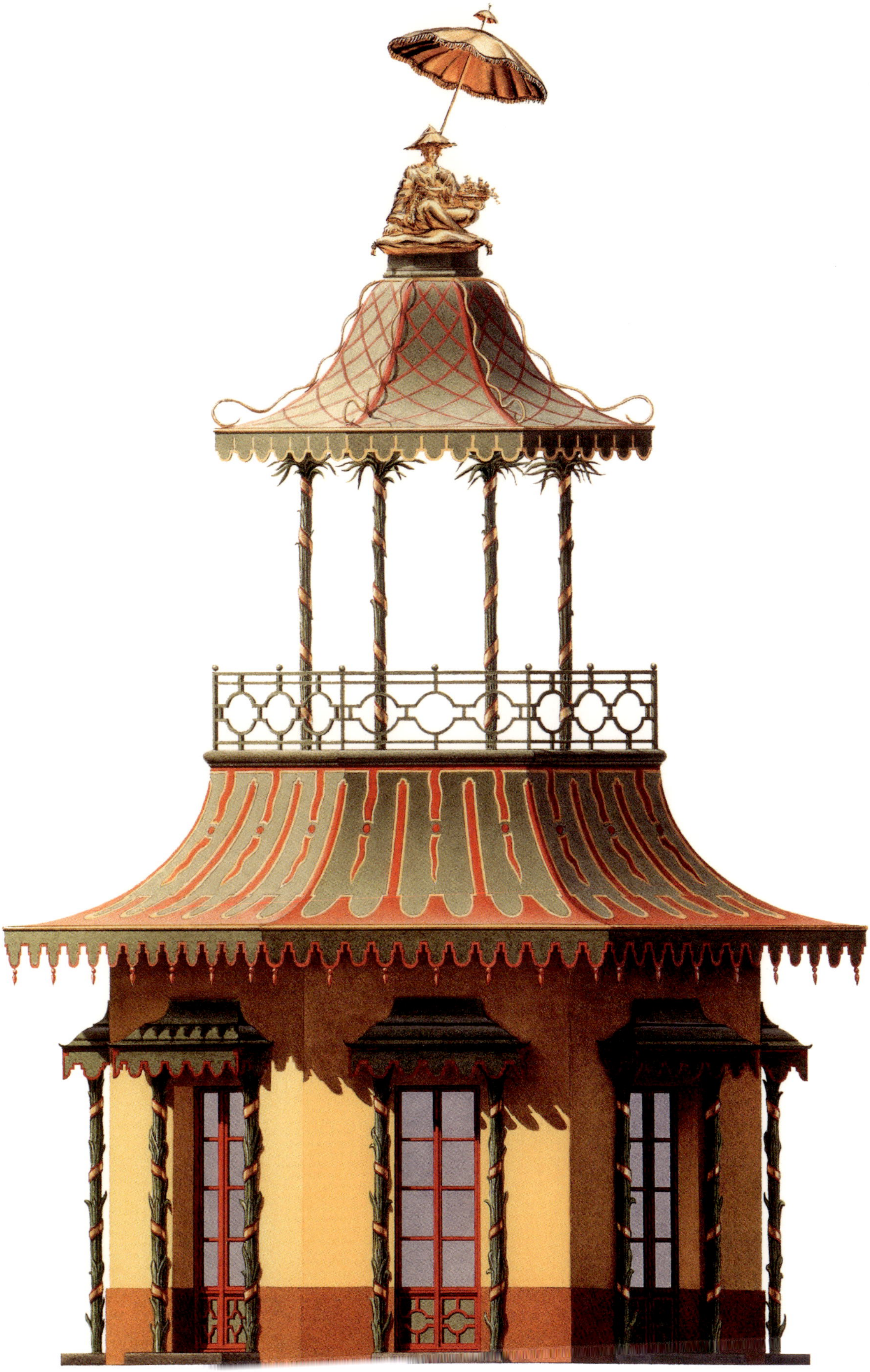

Chinese House at Désert de Retz

François Racine de Monville,
commissioner and architect
built 1777–1778
destroyed

Despite extreme losses, the Désert de Retz, near Chambourcy bordering the Forest of Marly, has gained a notoriety comparable to only one other, near-mythic garden, Bomarzo, with which it shares a rare quality of intense poetry and imagination. The creation of François Racine de Monville, a man favored with literally every talent and advantage, "de Monville's Wilderness" achieved rare fame among his contemporaries: Queen Marie-Antoinette, King Gustav III of Sweden and American ambassadors Thomas Jefferson and Benjamin Franklin would each make pilgrimages to meet its owner and view his extraordinary folly park.

The estate's physical and symbolic center was de Monville's residence, the Ruined Column, built in the early 1780s, which suggested the remnant of an incomprehensibly vast ancient monument. His original home and favored retreat was the Chinese House, a two-story teak pavilion built beside a small pond. The building's exterior featured faux-bamboo columns and intricately carved latticework panels and was animated by life-sized Chinese mannequins standing in niches and leaning over the upper balustrade. The Chinese House inspired a direct imitation in the gardens of Steinfurt, Germany, and also influenced projects initiated by Gustav III in Sweden.

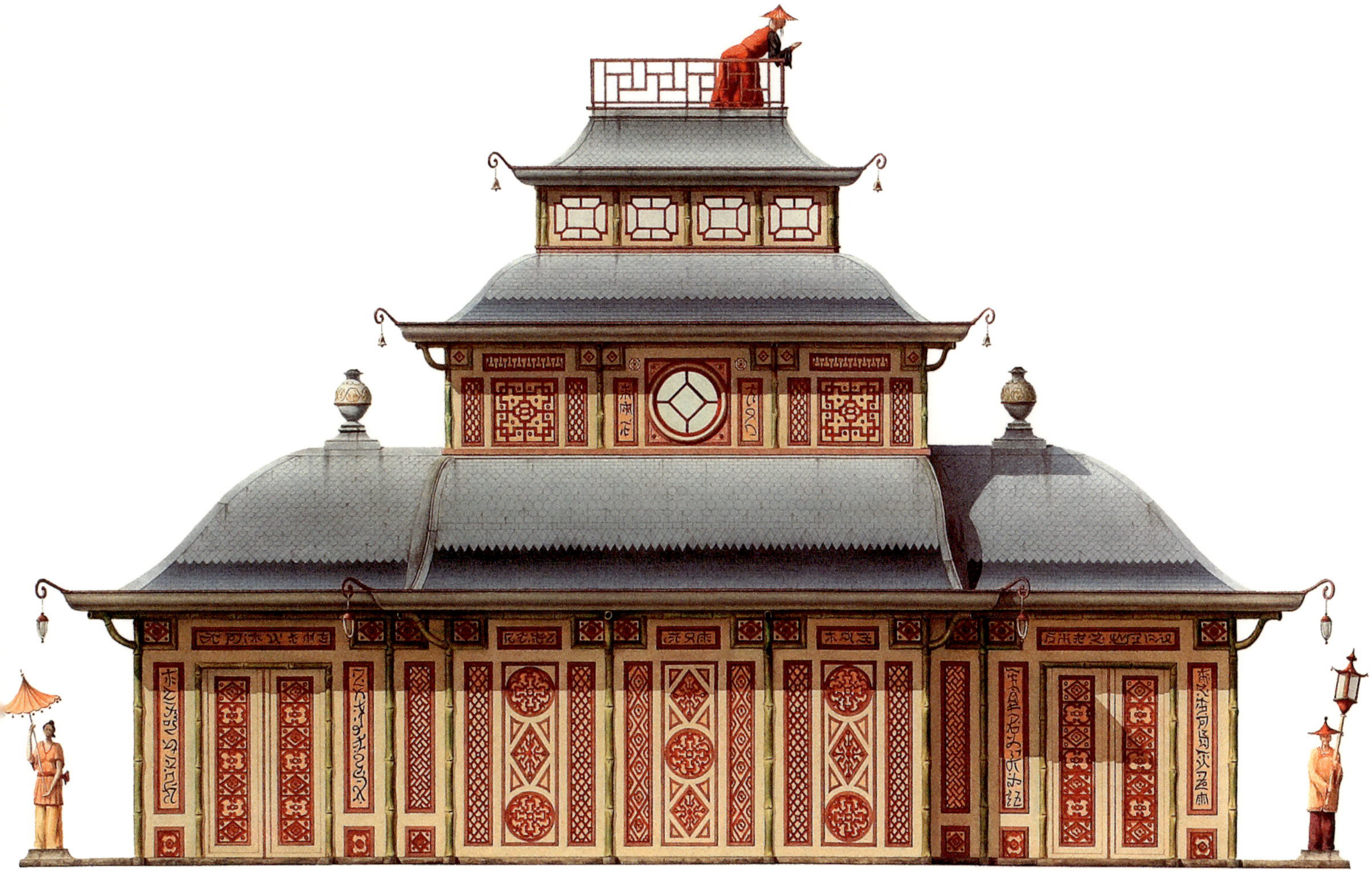

Chinese Gate House at Désert de Retz

François Racine de Monville,
commissioner and architect
built circa 1777
destroyed

Colorful, brash and naïve, the Chinese gate house at the Désert de Retz is the embodiment of a Chinoiserie garden folly and announced entry into the most remarkable garden of its time. Once over its threshold, the visitor found himself in the magic realm of Monsieur de Monville, who lived in a gigantic broken column in the center of a garden dotted with fantastic structures. To evoke the Orient, de Monville employed the traditional Chinoiserie color scheme of red, green and yellow introduced in the writings of the Dutch missionary John Nieuhoff a century earlier. To further transform the simple wooden hut, fanciful Chinese pictographs were painted on the walls and a wooden billboard with a faux-Chinese inscription was mounted against the sinuously curved roof.

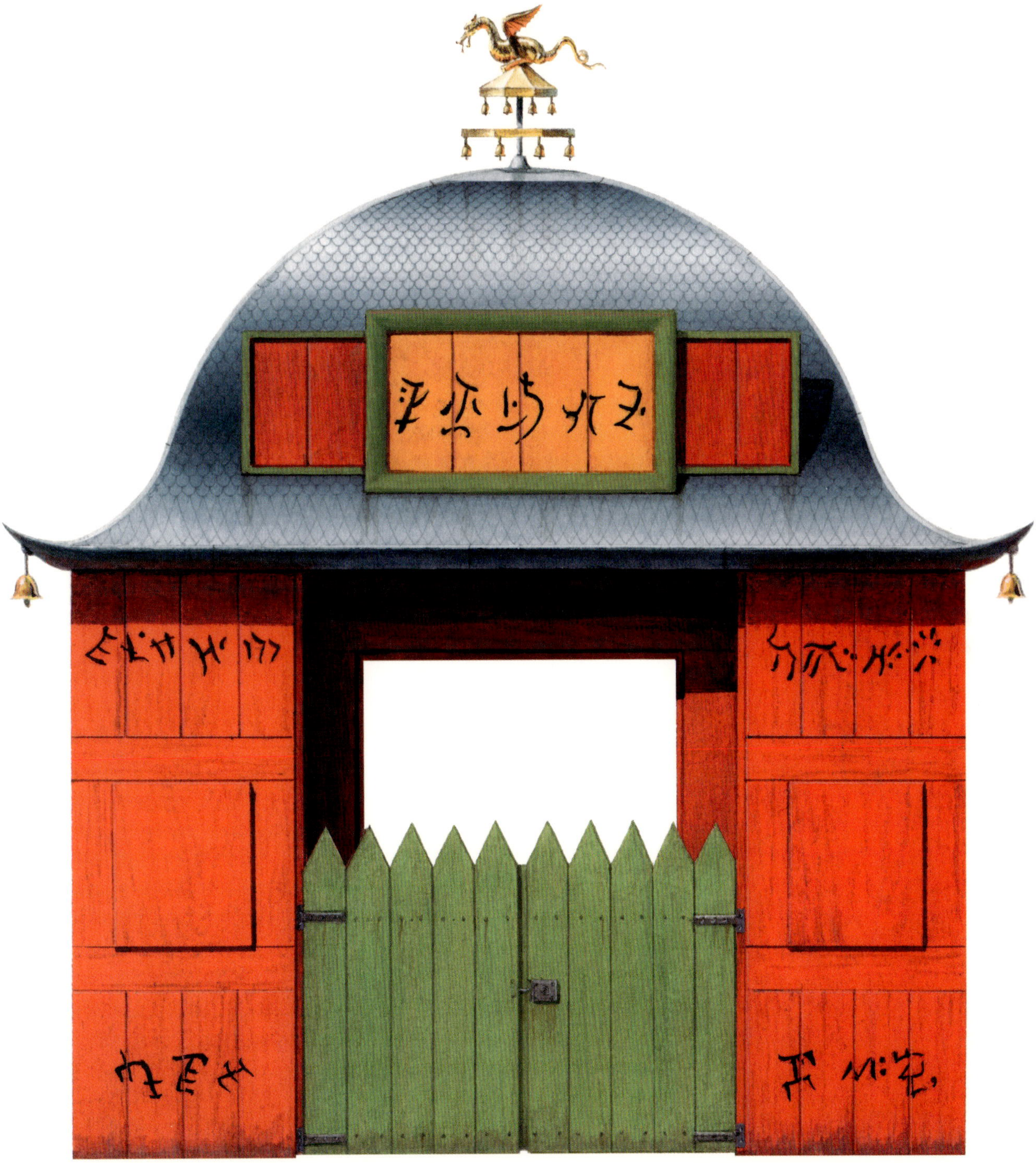

SIAMESE TENT AT DÉSERT DE RETZ

FRANÇOIS RACINE DE MONVILLE,
COMMISSIONER AND ARCHITECT
BUILT CIRCA 1778
DESTROYED; REBUILT 1989

THE SIAMESE TENT at Retz stands on the Island of Happiness in a wooded glade at the western edge of the Désert, and was reconstructed in 1989 as part of an ambitious restoration program. The Tartar Tent at Parc Monceau (*p. 51*), which Carmontelle designed some three years earlier, almost certainly served as de Monville's inspiration. "Made in the Siamese fashion" and originally used to store arms, the tent is sheathed in metal sheets and painted in trompe-loeil representing striped canvas; its entrance is framed with illusionistic swags and a central skylight illuminates an interior formerly hung with toile de Jouy.

After his visit in 1784, Gustav III of Sweden requested documentation of the Désert and wrote to de Monville upon receiving it: "I believe that anyone with taste cannot but applaud the whole and the details of your plan"; drawings of the Siamese Tent would directly inspire the famed Chinese Tent in his gardens at Haga.

*Following pages: a view of the pagoda of Schoonenberg at Laeken,
today destroyed, by an unknown artist.*

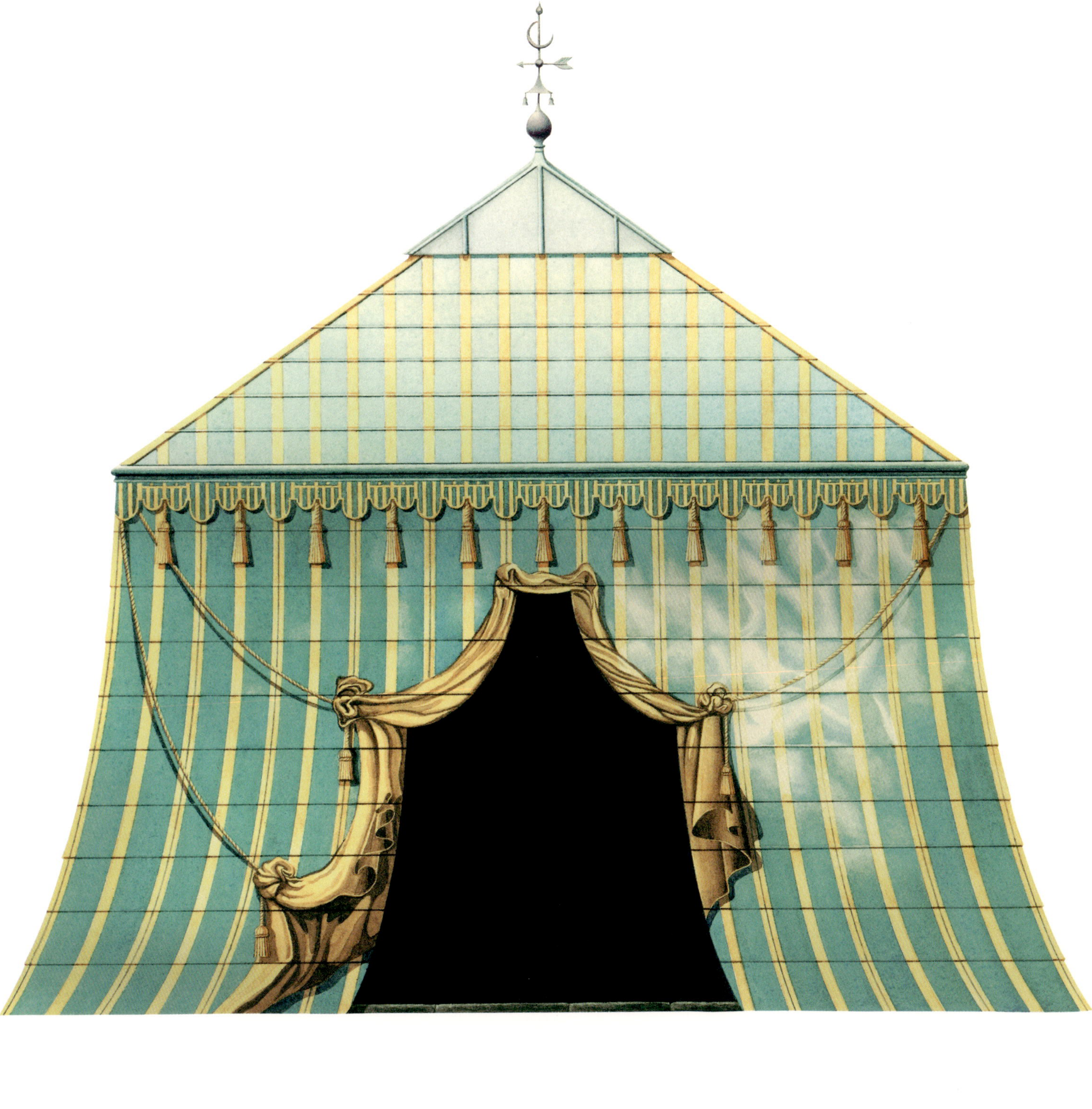

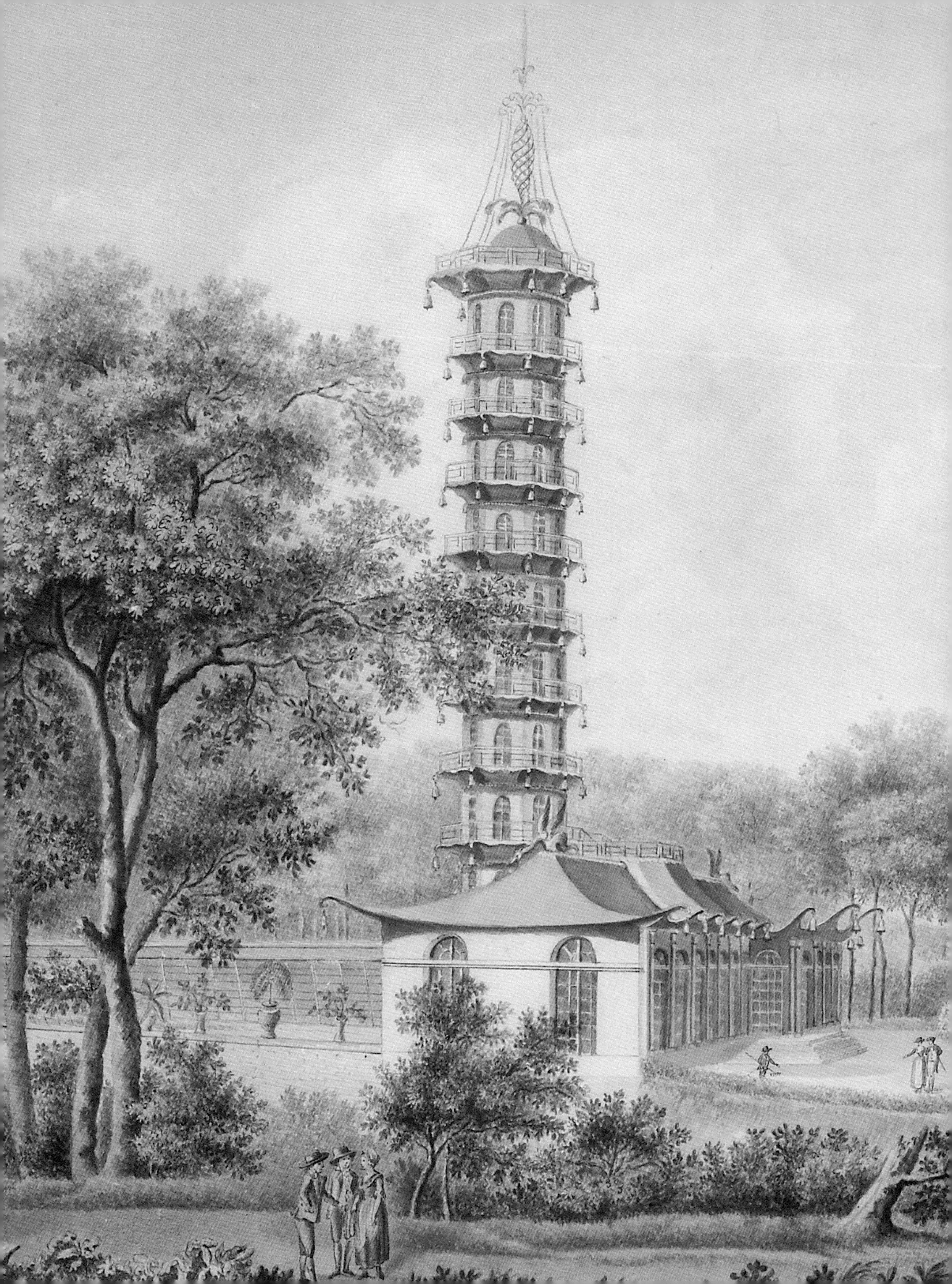

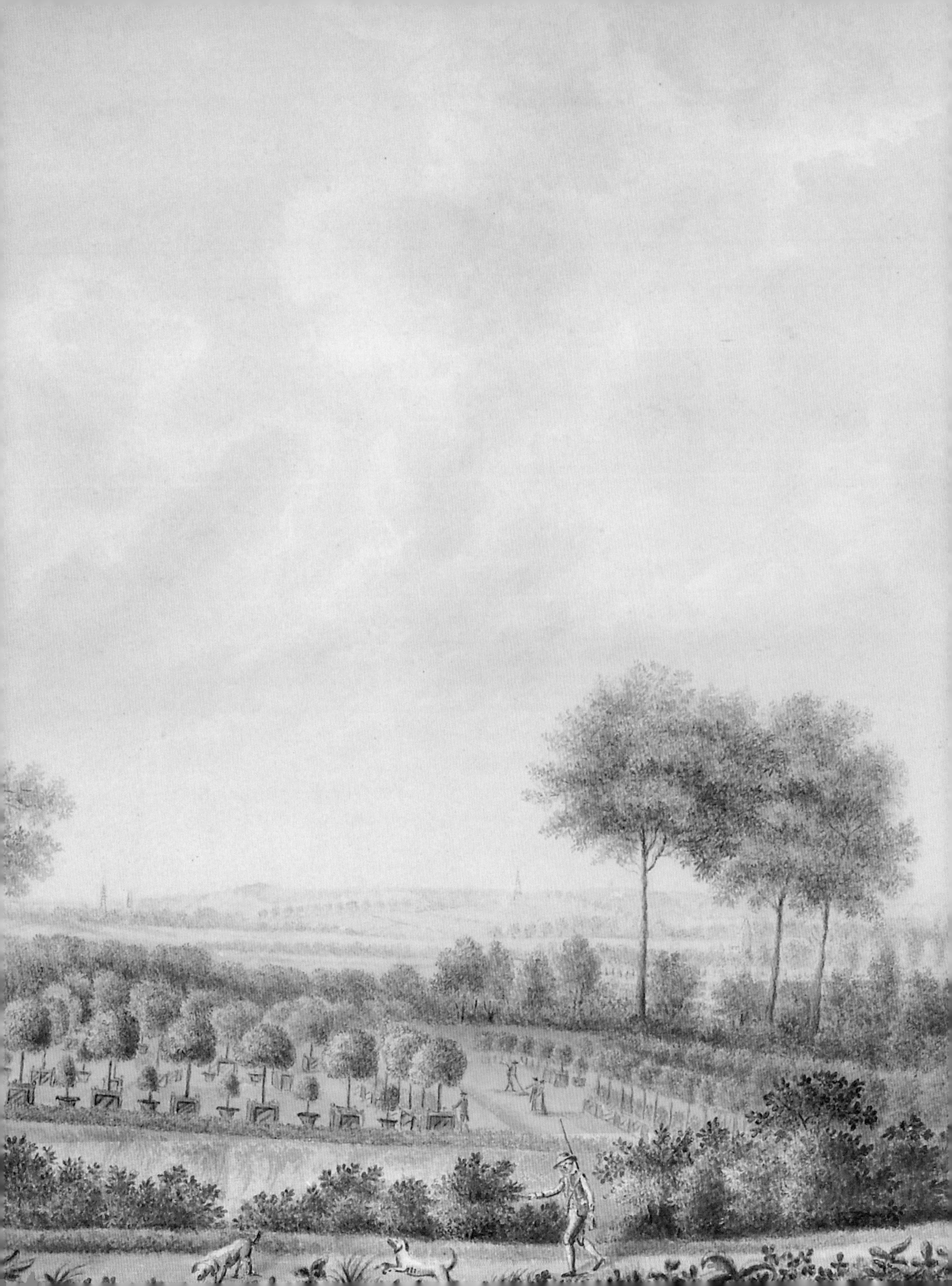

Pagoda at Chanteloup

Duc de Choiseul, commissioner
Louis-Denis de Camus, architect
built 1778
extant

CHANTELOUP, a large Loire Valley estate near Amboise, was the amusement of the Duc de Choiseul, minister to Louis XV, after his fall from near-total power over the affairs of France. Exiled from Versailles in 1770, Choiseul enlarged the château, installed wife and mistress, built a grandiose classical garden just as they were falling irrevocably out of fashion, then remade the grounds a few years later in the latest *anglo-chinois* style. The pagoda, originally conceived as "a bauble of a thousand *louis*, finally cost him forty thousand *ecus*, a sum he shrugged off," noted the Comte de Cheverny. A bankrupt in all but name, the duke celebrated the pagoda's completion in April 1778 with the expected panache, and the great stone exclamation mark became as much a monument to his own audacity as to the loyalty of the friends he wished to honor.

The tower, the work of the architect Louis-Denis de Camus, a curious amalgam of French classicism and unorthodox detailing, faithfully reprised a design for a pagoda published by Le Rouge in 1775 (*p. 136*)—itself an interpretation of Sir William Chambers' famed pagoda at Kew (*pp. 92-93*). The ground floor, a Doric rotunda, echoes the temple of Vesta; the second floor was conceived as a salon, and dinners would be held with a light orchestra playing on the floor above. Marble plaques listing the duke's friends and thanking them for their fidelity in exile are mounted on the walls of the ground floor.

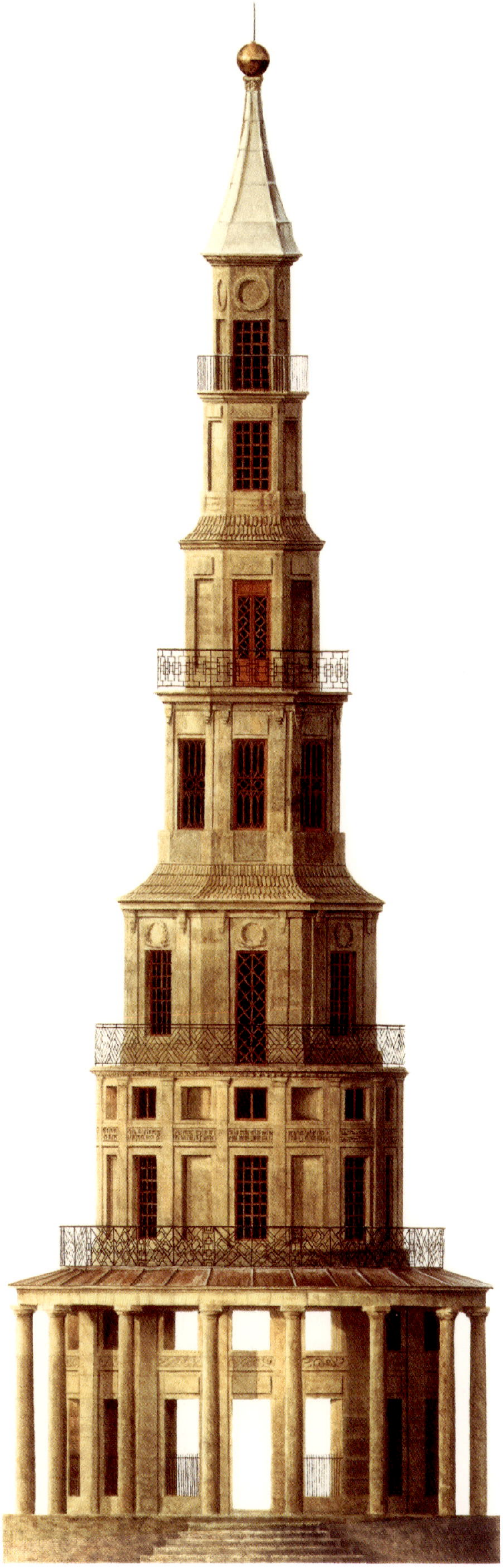

Chinese Tent at Bagatelle

Comte d'Artois, commissioner
François-Joseph Bélanger, architect
built circa 1778
destroyed

THE STORY OF BAGATELLE could be an ancien régime fairy tale: the Comte d'Artois, youngest brother to Louis XVI and barely twenty years old, having just purchased the estate and wanting to rebuild it without undue expense, wagered Marie-Antoinette 100,000 *livres* that he could reconstruct Bagatelle before the end of the court's autumn voyage to Fontainebleau. The count diverted building materials entering the gates of Paris to the worksite—to great public outcry—where nine hundred laborers worked by torchlight through the autumn nights. Sixty-four days later, on November 25, 1777, the new Bagatelle was completed, though the queen would not inaugurate it until the following spring and her payment would but begin to defray its three-million-*livre* cost.

The Chinese Tent at Bagatelle, along with a handsome Chinese Bridge, was the complement to the Philosopher's Pavilion (*p. 87*) and in many ways its inversion—open wherever it was solid, and indeed so delicately ephemeral it seemed barely moored to the ground. The fretwork pavilion was built on a rectangular platform raised on stilts, where guests could enjoy an elevated view as well as refreshments. Its theatricality and insubstantiality are emblematic of the garden structures of the period, which were often no more than passing fancies made tangible—thrown together in a day, they were intended to survive no longer than the smiles they imparted.

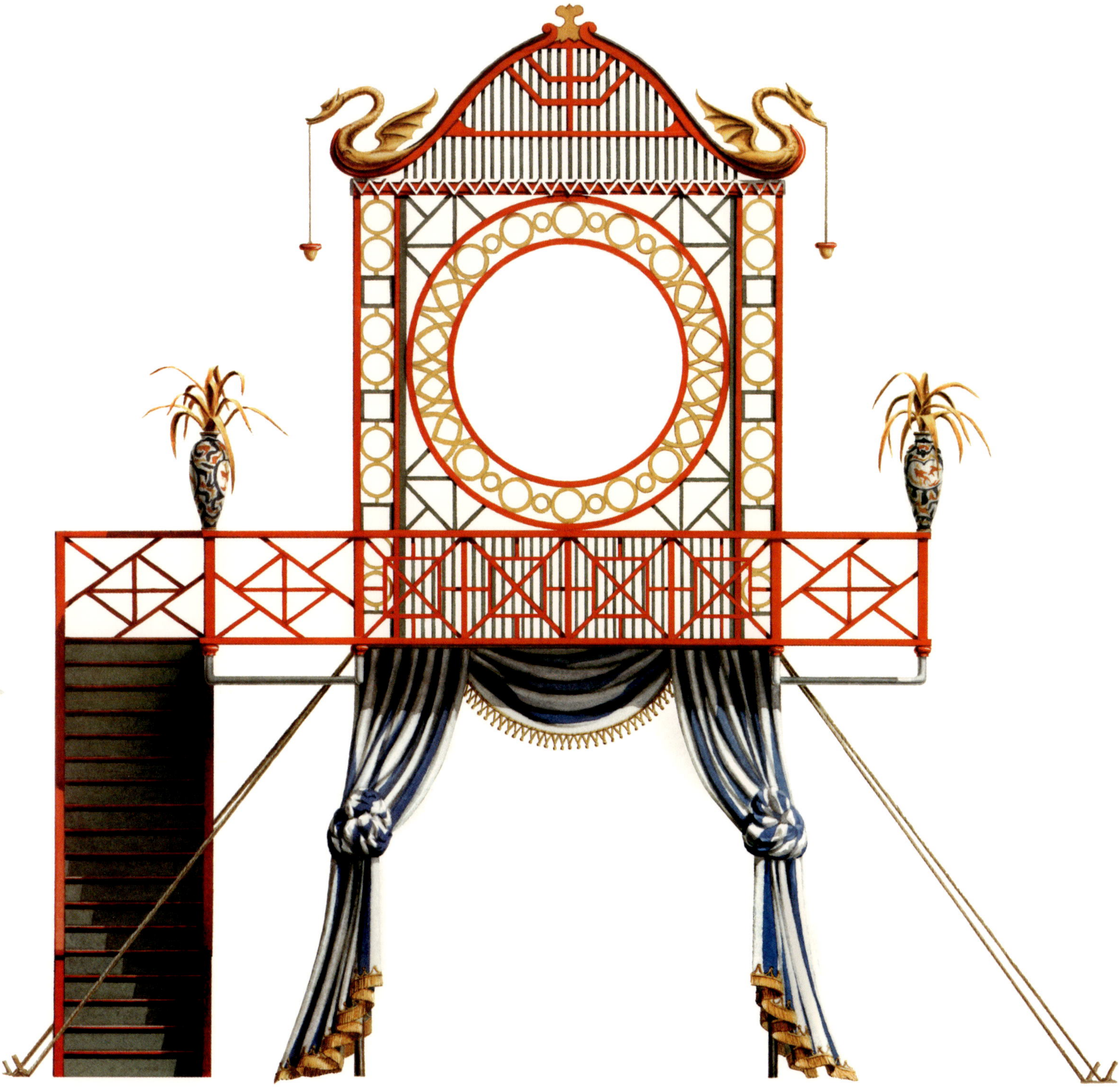

Philosopher's Pavilion at Bagatelle

Comte d'Artois, commissioner
François-Joseph Bélanger, architect
built circa 1778
destroyed

The Bagatelle Gardens, less absurdly charged than those of the Folie Sainte-James, featured a full repertoire of follies spanning the world's cultures, with Chinoiserie structures predominating. The Philosopher's Pavilion was certainly the most charming construction, a small octagonal kiosk perched atop a rockwork grotto. A contemporary guidebook described its setting: "Here is a small lake surrounded by rocks, poplars and willows, whose branches droop over the water. A bridge connects the little island with an enclosed bosquet in the midst of which rises a hollow rock, surmounted by a little Gothic building called The Philosopher's Hut. From the balcony running around this small building one enjoys several beautiful and fascinating views."

The pavilion was a composite of Gothic, rustic and Chinoiserie elements, and its interior was adorned with medallions of Greek philosophers, and "its windows were composed of multicolored glass, through which one views Nature with diverse tints, the emblems of human passions, which make men see different colors in the same object." The grotto beneath offered seats from which to contemplate a ceiling "tapestry of seemingly all the most agreeable minerals: without a doubt the natural history cabinet of a philosopher, just as the pavilion above is his observatory." Period sources indicate the structure was predominantly yellow.

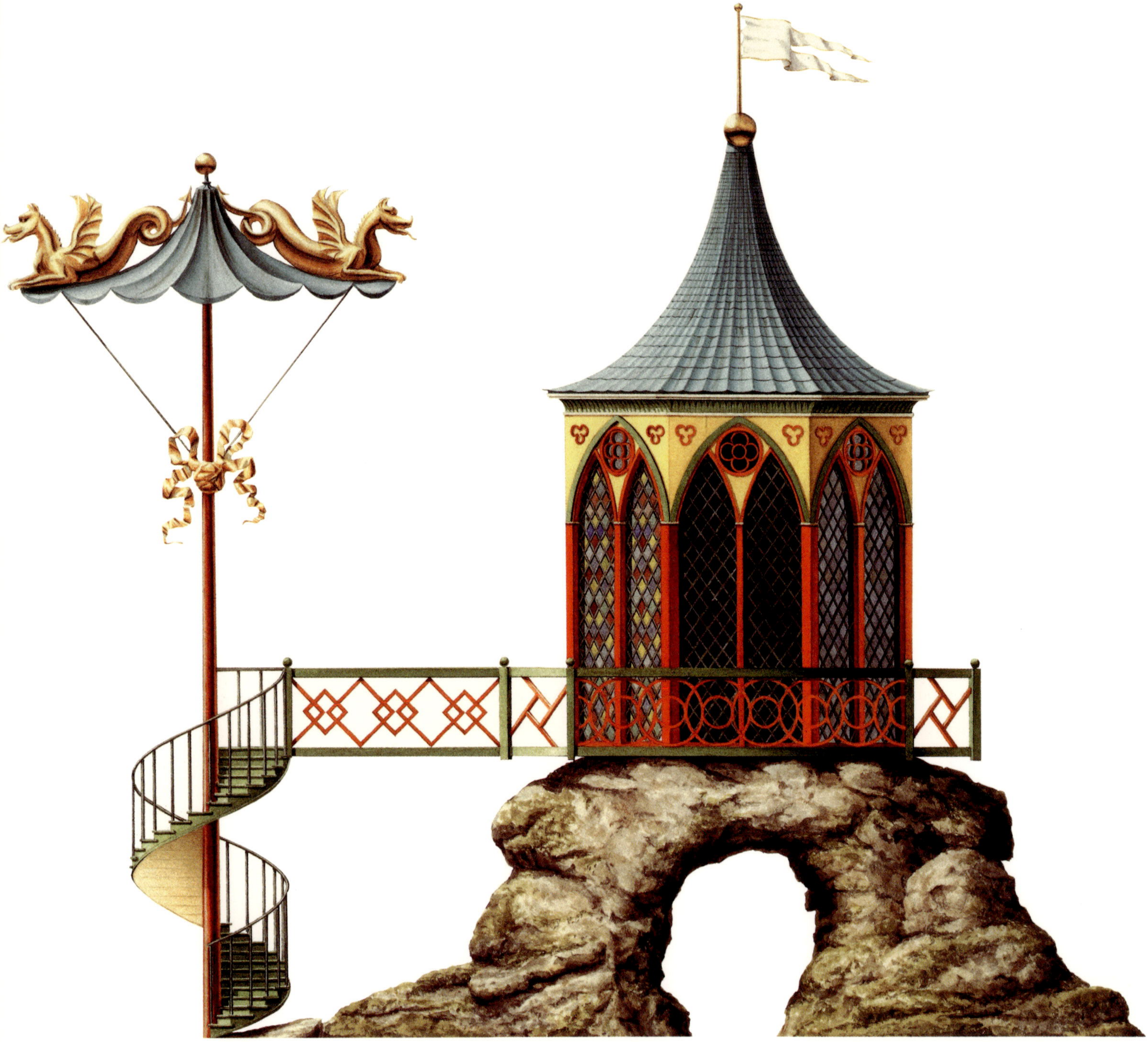

Chinese Tent after Georges Le Rouge

Anonymous Architect
Published 1779

GEORGES LE ROUGE published an engraving of this and the following tent in 1779 in the seventh album of *Détail des nouveaux jardins à la mode*, naming them kiosks and claiming that they stood in the Imperial gardens of Yuan-Ming Yuan, a remarkable inversion of Chinoiserie—an extensive rococo palace complex and gardens designed by the Italian architect Père Giuseppe Castiglione for the Chinese emperor. He also noted they were "in the taste of those at Mortefontaine," an estate in the Oise near Ermenonville, and though it is impossible to corroborate either assertion, stylistically the tents are perfectly in keeping with the unbridled rococo exuberance of Castiglione's work in China.

Europeans in the eighteenth century considered tents the most characteristic of Oriental structures and indiscriminately described them as Tartar, Turkish or Chinese. As picturesque as they were inexpensive, tents were a staple element of Anglo-Chinese folly gardens and a number of them, such as the Tartar Tent at the Parc Monceau (*p. 51*) and the Siamese Tent at the Désert de Retz (*p. 79*), were even constructed of permanent materials.

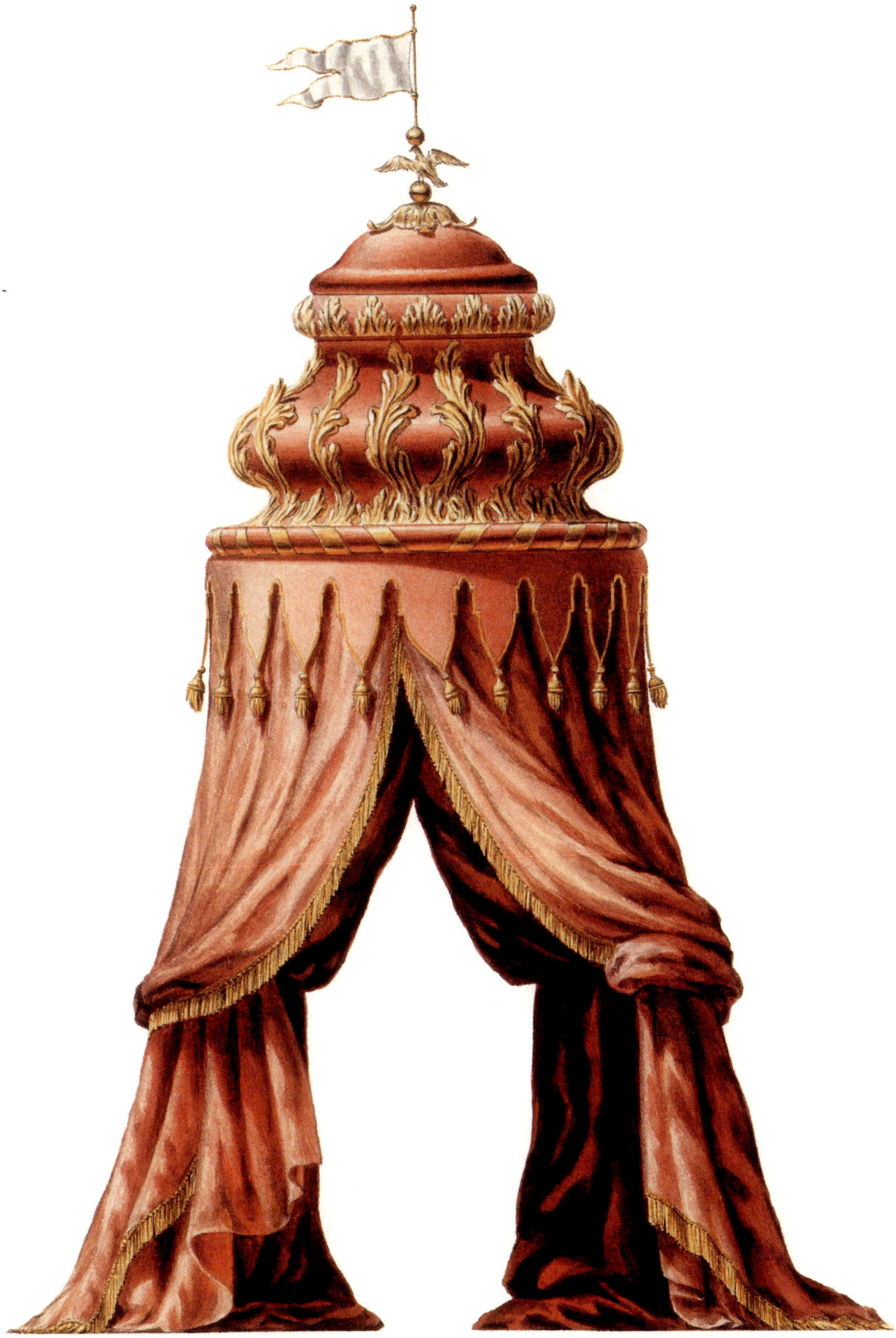

Chinese Tent after Georges Le Rouge

Anonymous Architect
published 1779

The pair of tents depicted here again illustrates the influence of George Le Rouge's *Détail des nouveaux jardins à la mode*, as virtual copies were erected in the Bagno gardens at Steinfurt, Westphalia, by the Prince zu Bentheim und Steinfurt. The prince pillaged Le Rouge's earlier plates to people the Bagno, a cluttered but charmingly naïve folly park of remarkable pretension given such a provincial location.

In a curious tautology, Le Rouge then published extensive plans and views of the Bagno in his final album, creating a visual echo chamber of his own influence. Named "*Illuminations chinoises*," the tents stood at one end of a large oval parterre, flanking an alley leading to a treillage arcade and facing a small concert hall. A copy of the Chinese House at the Désert de Retz (*p. 75*) stood at the midpoint of the oval and, to complete the stylistic chaos, faced a Gothic banqueting room opposite. Almost the entirety of the follies at the Bagno were lost with time save the concert hall, built of durable materials and recently restored.

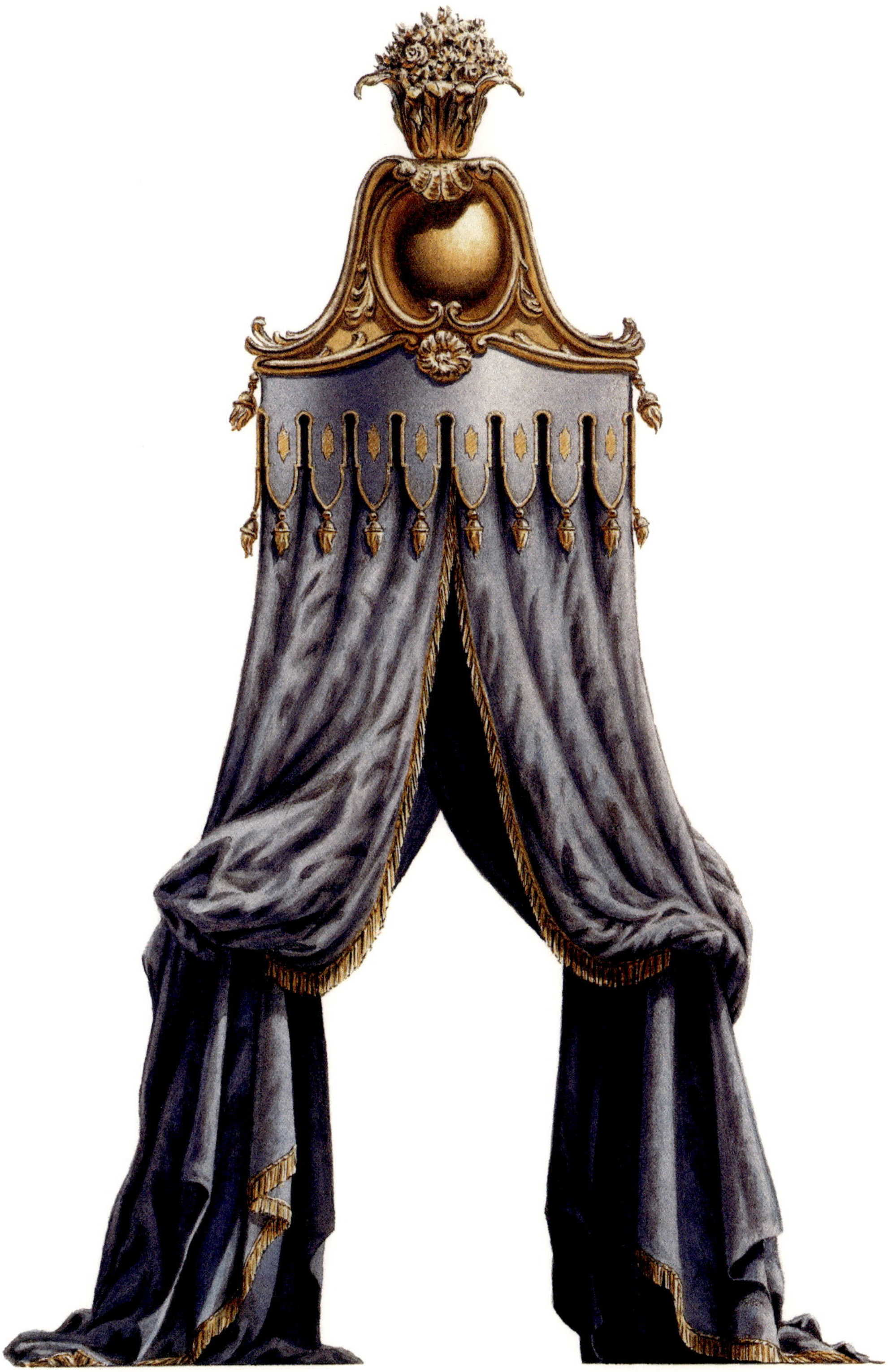

Sir William Chambers

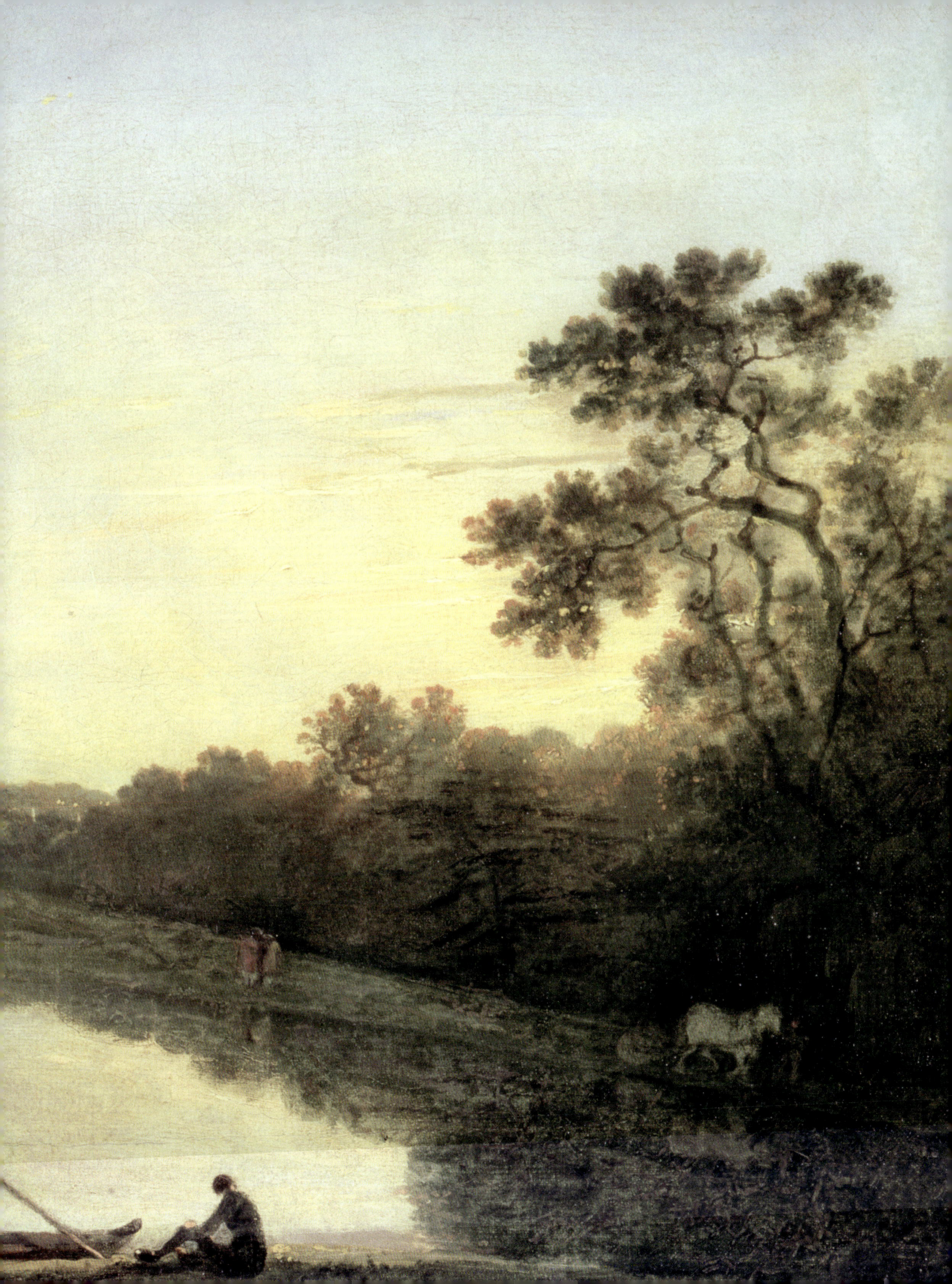

Previous pages: Kew Gardens: The Pagoda and Bridge *by Richard Wilson.*

Sir William Chambers

THE ENGLISH ARCHITECT Sir William Chambers is a seminal figure in the history of the Chinoiserie style and the impact of his buildings and publications cannot be underestimated, though they are but a portion of his remarkable body of work. More than any other figure, he shaped both the intellectual content and the outward appearance of the Anglo-Chinese landscape garden and the innumerable pagodas animating them. His extraordinary career began inconspicuously enough. Born to affluent Scottish parents living in Sweden, he set out, barely seventeen years old, on his first voyage to Bengal as a member of the Swedish East India Company in 1740. Intending to become a merchant seaman, he then journeyed to Canton in 1743, and it was there that he began to study Chinese architecture—an interest he continued to pursue during his third and final voyage, returning to Europe in 1748.

Financially independent and equipped with a trove of notes on Chinese manners, as well as sketches and drawings, Chambers reinvented himself as the foremost European authority on Chinese building and design, cultivating a wide network of friends and foes alike to further his position. A journey to Paris to study architecture under Jean-François Blondel at the École des Arts acquainted him with the theories of the leading architects of his time and further burnished his stature. The obligatory Roman sojourn followed, where he and his wife cleverly found quarters next door to the Piranesi family, through whom he gained access to the international art cognoscenti.

Like so many architects before and after, Chambers mastered society as a means to professional advancement. His path to celebrity as one of Europe's foremost architects was paved with countless letters of recommendation and introduction, though vicious denunciations circulated nearly as freely. In 1755,

Chinoiseries

Chambers returned to London, famous but unemployed. Assessing his situation, he embarked upon a publicity venture that would subsequently secure him his first royal commission, at Kew gardens for the Dowager Princess Augusta. Until then he had been known as a highly talented theorist, and the gardens and exotic follies he created at Kew would bring him major commissions and lasting fame.

Publication of his *The Design of Chinese Buildings* in 1757 opened the final, frenetic chapter in the Chinoiserie craze. Before Chambers, the Jesuit Father Matteo Ripa had written one of the first descriptions of Chinese landscaping, an account of the emperor's garden at Jehol, created in 1713, and another Jesuit, Father Jean-Denis Attiret, published an influential account of the imperial summer palace of Yuan-Ming Yuan in 1749, with an English translation following three years later. Attiret had fallen under the spell of Chinese aesthetics, and his translation of the palace's allusive name, Perfect Clarity, was in pointed opposition to its exuberant conflation of the European Baroque with Chinese architecture. "Everything here is grand and truly beautiful in design and execution," he remarked, and slyly noted that the Chinese, viewing engravings of western architecture, compared European streets to mountain chasms; houses and castles resembled cliffs pierced with caves, more appropriate as dwellings for bears than men.

Nonetheless it was the authoritative tone of *The Design of Chinese Buildings* that reverberated across Europe. Chambers had relied heavily on these and other earlier writings, distilling them with his own materials into a seemingly informed essay that, allied with his revelatory plates, was a major contribution to the theoretical and visual foundations of the Anglo-Chinese garden and the Chinoiserie style. Chambers followed the success of his first book with a splendid portfolio

Sir William Chambers

of the architecture of Kew gardens, published in 1763, further cementing his prominence as master of foreign styles. The plates became another influential sourcebook, and as late as 1795, with the pagoda at Oranienbaum, near Wörlitz, garden follies were erected copying his designs at Kew.

Chambers published *The Design of Chinese Buildings*, with its illustrious dedication to the Prince of Wales, just as the initial mania for Chinoiserie was faltering in England, and he saw its purpose as a corrective to its excesses—"to put a stop to the extravagancies that daily appear under the name of Chinese"—a goal the volume certainly fulfilled. With its seeming authenticity, the treatise proffered a new, more sober academic approach to the subject: for the first time, Chinese architecture was treated as a serious subject in its own right and not simply as an amusing means to animate picturesque scenery—though ironically this was exactly what Chambers would later recommend.

While he mistook the Cantonese style as representative of Chinese architecture as a whole, Chambers' observations and drawings were executed from an architect's viewpoint, and he was the first to provide accurate, if not always genuine, details of architectural elements such as column bases and roof trusses. Of a sudden a normative pattern book became available, carefully edited for the European market, that allowed designers to assemble Chinoiserie follies from different parts and ideas, apparently guaranteeing authentic Chinese buildings in Western gardens. (There was ample reason for skepticism; in addition to his own sources, Chambers had urgently requested additional drawings from his brother in Gothenburg only months before publication.) Chambers couched his text as a firsthand account by one of Europe's foremost architectural theoreticians, declaring Chinese architecture, after close study, to be inferior to that of antiquity and,

Chinoiseries

lacking applicable rules, to be inappropriate for Europe except to create charming garden scenes—an echo of Sir William Temple's observation that "graceful disorder reigned delightfully in Chinese gardens."

Though the book's impact was minor in England, where Chinoiserie was already in irrevocable decline, Chambers' vision fell on particularly fertile ground in France. With the legacy of Le Nôtre also waning, his treatise was enormously influential in shaping the idea of the new Anglo-Chinese garden and his plates became the visual sourcebook for the majority of Chinoiserie buildings erected in the last decades before the French Revolution.

While the writings of Jean-Jacques Rousseau had an equally important impact in popularizing the idea of the picturesque and in shaping the conception of the Anglo-Chinese garden in France—he famously elevated a garden stroll into a metaphysical promenade by declaring, "Our foremost teachers of philosophy are our feet, hands and eyes"—Rousseau nonetheless critiqued the Chinese garden as "nature wearing a thousand disguises, none of them natural." However, it was exactly this artifice that appealed to French sensibilities, and his dictum "There is no sin of which they [the Chinese] are not proud" was hardly a notion to discomfit the French nobility.

The vast, pastoral English landscape conceived by Capability Brown never found favor in France, where lots were typically small and enclosed by walls, but Chambers' vision of the studied disarray of the *jardin anglo-chinois* became the intellectual and aesthetic engine driving France's unfolding garden mania. As

Opposite: Chinese temple designs, engraved by Georges Le Rouge, after Sir William Chambers.

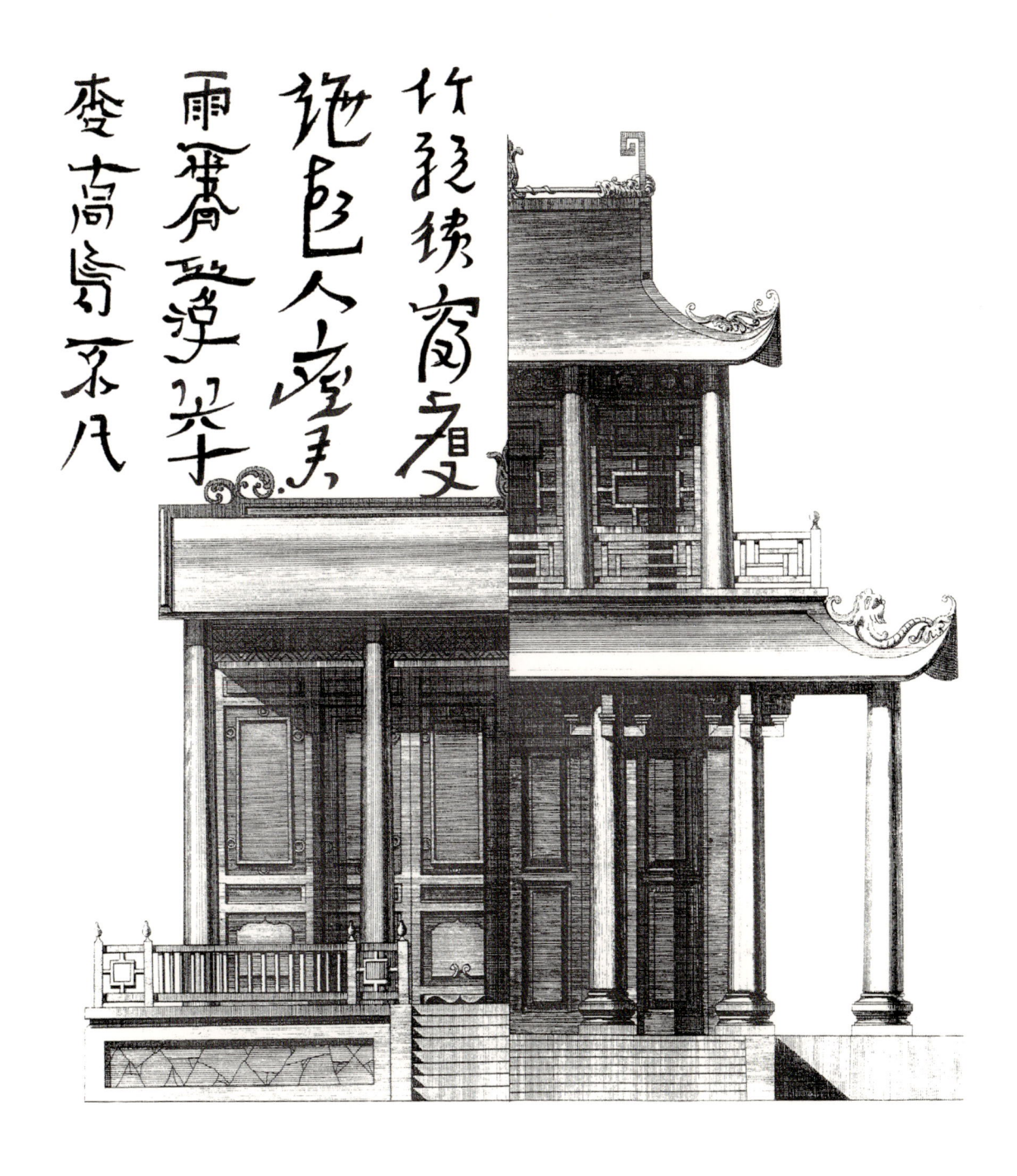

Sir William Chambers

Chinoiseries

Hirschfeld explained the impetus, "The Englishman in the country looks for rural pleasures. The Frenchman takes the town into the country with him. The Englishman is himself a gardener and cultivator of his garden. The Frenchman is seldom more than a decorator." His judgment was later seconded by Pierre Cuisin, who maliciously captured his countrymen's new esprit: "What a marvelous country! […] From an elegant kiosk limn your edifice, atop plaster rocks with a rocaille soul, a pasteboard grotto of graceful profile. So does the Parisian, cane in hand, leave his house to stroll in Canton."

Pride soon entered the picture and a spirited debate arose as a host of garden theoreticians and aristocratic dilettantes on both sides of the Channel debated the sources and comparative merits of the French and English approach to the picturesque landscape garden. In rapid succession Claude-Henri Watelet, Horace Walpole, André Duchesne, Jean-Marie Morel, Jean-Jacques Rousseau, Thomas Whately, the Prince de Ligne, the Marquis de Girardin and the Duc d'Harcourt weighed in, carrying on a spirited intellectual brawl throughout the 1770s. Predictably, the polemic split along national lines; Walpole stated categorically that the English "have given the true model of the art of gardening to the world," lauding the originality and simple elegance so characteristic of English landscape gardens.

Watelet's pronouncements were typical of the French stance: "This nation [England] is said to have borrowed the idea of its gardens from the Chinese, a people living too far away, and too different from ourselves not to be the occasion of extraordinary opinions and many fables." The Duc d'Harcourt opined, "There are only two kinds of gardens, those which have been created by the Chinese, and those which have been created by the French…the English imitate what appeals

Sir William Chambers

to their taste without creating." For the Prince de Ligne there was no doubt that "When I use the expression 'the English garden' one should remember that this is a conventional phrase; for in truth it is the Chinese garden. It is evident…that the English owe their fame to the Chinese. It was the Chinese who first introduced the familiar waterfalls, felicitous chasms, horrors full of charm, grottoes, ruins and vantage points."

However, a few French iconoclasts entered the fray, such as Morel, who wrote in 1776, "Let us express our gratitude to this nation [England] for having restored to Nature her inviolable rights and to art its true principles." The Prince de Ligne, a hopeless contrarian, took delight in contradicting himself and his adopted countrymen by writing, "Gardens are now being designed in France under the name *chino-anglais* or *anglo-chinois*, for one cannot distinguish between these two elements. The French might have had such gardens before the English, if their missionaries had not been so preoccupied with their consciences and commerce. They overlooked more interesting things and brought to Paris nothing but wallpaper, screens and caricatures, which have been used in various pavilions and ridiculous ballets. The English appropriated everything, even the furniture, the simplicity, the finesse, the purity—a valuable conquest."

Despite strenuous French protestations of English appropriation, it was obvious that the French appropriation was twice removed, and Hirschfeld, standing on the sidelines in Germany, summarized the French defeat with Teutonic bluntness: "In their blind imitation of the English taste they not only repeat its faults but also add new ones of their own. Everything that a large park can contain is crowded into an area not exceeding half an acre. Everything that Asia can offer in the way

Chinoiseries

of new varieties of trees must be copied in a spot measuring a few hundred steps in circumference. Chinese monstrosities and kiosks, the freakish features of this new, extravagant architecture, have ousted the pure simplicity of the Greek."

Lost in the heat of debate, though it did nothing to favor the French position, was a crucial distinction the English made between their landscaped parks and landscape gardens. Rightly, the most perceptive English writers identified the landscape park of Capability Brown as a native invention, inspired by, if anything, the classical landscapes painted by Claude and Rosa and described by Pliny, and the picturesque landscape garden, also first cultivated in England, as having its inspiration in these former gardens, with a nod to the influence of Sharawadgi. Though hostile to Brown, Chambers would make exactly this point in *A Dissertation on Chinese Gardening* in 1772. In fact, Chinese gardens were rarities and apart from Yuan-Ming Yuan, extremely constricted affairs; moreover, no illustrations reached European eyes until Georges Le Rouge's plates of that garden circulated in the late 1780s, as the debate over origins and influence waned. The great fault of the French *jardin anglo-chinois* was its conflation of the two, a reductio ad absurdum of both styles that led to such farcically dense amusement parks as the Parc Monceau (*pp. 51, 53*) and the Folie Sainte-James (*pp. 139, 141*).

The controversial *A Dissertation on Chinese Gardening* was Chambers' third major publication on Chinese architecture and gardens. Keenly attuned to the intellectual pulse of his time and the growing interest in naturalism, Chambers launched the *Dissertation* as a thinly veiled polemic aimed at his nemesis, Lancelot

Opposite: Bridge in a Garden in Canton *by Georges Le Rouge, after Sir William Chambers.*

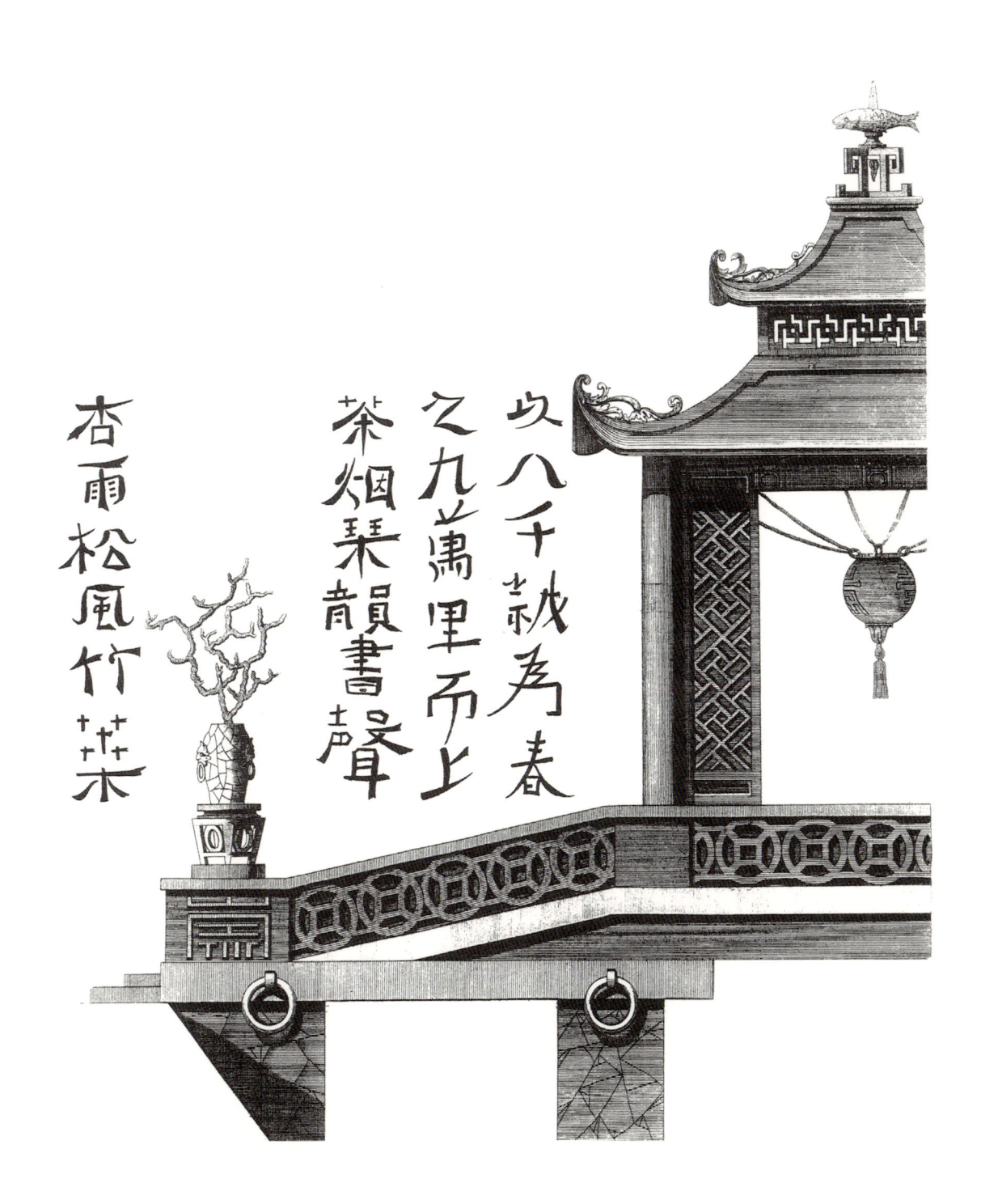

Sir William Chambers

以八千歲為春
之九萬里而上
茶烟琴韻書聲

杏雨松風竹葉

Chinoiseries

"Capability" Brown, who had won a commission Chambers coveted to landscape the country seat of Lord Clive. Brown's approach to landscape was minimalist: the gardener's efforts should enhance the site's natural attributes and be imperceptible. Chambers believed man's interventions superior to nature: the garden was a human construct, a work of art, and his signature should be evident. He praised the Chinese for taking nature as their template, to be improved by cunning artifice, thereby creating a striking union of nature and art. Liberally citing fictitious quotations from Chinese sages that even gullible readers found dubious, he described numerous gardens that imitated nature in all its beautiful irregularity and stressed the impulses and emotions they sparked in the mind and soul.

  Though he did not mention him by name, Chambers dismissed Brown's achievement as "gardens which differ little from common fields" and asserted that perfection could be achieved only by creating a diversity of scenes to captivate and entertain the visitor. Years later he claimed the true intent of his "little book," as he fondly called the *Dissertation*, had been to offer an introduction to Chinese architecture, but by then his interpretations had become fact, his engravings iconic and his recommendations gospel for gardeners across the Continent.

The apparent rigor of Chambers' publications, antithetical to the whimsical concoctions of the day, ensured them extraordinary success and reinvigorated Chinoiserie, though within Chambers' academic posturing lay the seeds of the style's demise. Much as efforts by Claude Perrault and the Académie Royale to codify classical architecture under Louis XIV led to a sterile, formulaic neoclassicism that ultimately expired in its academic straitjacket, so the myriad imitators derived from Chambers' plates rapidly exhausted the creative potential of his material.

Sir William Chambers

Chinese personnages by Georges Le Rouge, after Sir William Chambers.

The backlash came quickly. In large part due to their very ubiquity, Chinoiserie follies fell precipitously from fashion in the 1780s, but *The Design of Chinese Buildings* also played a major role, having snuffed out the essential life source of Chinoiserie, the realm of imagination. As revolution approached, fickle tastemakers began plundering the world and its cultures in search of hitherto untapped ornamental possibilities. Voltaire noted happily, "I have everything in my garden…the groomed and the savage," and by 1781 the Prince de Ligne, who said, "One doesn't need money for anything. I make all my temples and suits on credit," would remark, "Chinese buildings reek of the boulevards and sideshow fairs," and sensed that "Gothic houses, too, are becoming too common." He proposed instead Moldavian huts and allowed that Arab and Turkish styles had not yet been exhausted.

Refreshment Tent for Versailles

Menus Plaisirs du Roi, commissioner
anonymous architect
designed 1779
unbuilt project

Ephemeral garden tents became extremely fashionable during the reign of Louis XVI, as their ease of construction, theatricality and low cost made them the perfect foil for the numerous, equally extravagant fêtes hosted by Marie-Antoinette. Rumor was such that after the Parisian mob stormed Versailles in 1789, deputies of the Third Estate demanded to see the queen's tents because they believed they were woven of precious fabrics encrusted with gold and silver. The reality was quite the contrary, more worthy of the stage than royalty: stick-and-lathe frames draped with painted canvas and hung with pasteboard decorations.

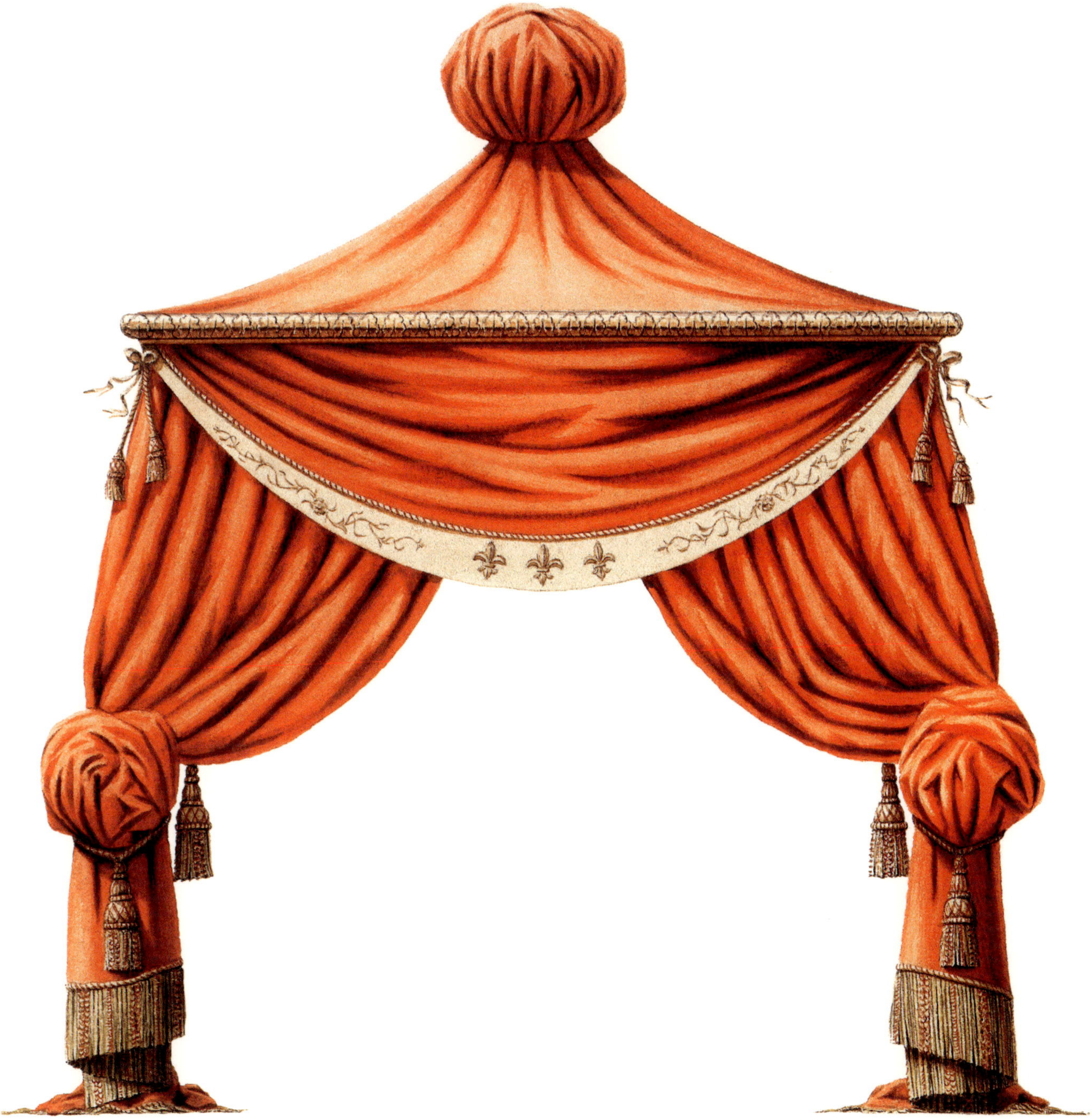

Refreshment Tent for Versailles

Menus Plaisirs du Roi, commissioner
anonymous architect
designed 1779
unbuilt project

This extravagantly caparisoned tent—one of an identical pair—and its smaller pendant illustrated previously were designed as refreshment stands to be placed before the garden façade of the Café de la Comédie for a fête given in 1779 in the town of Versailles. A notation on the original drawing records that the Director of the Menus Plaisirs du Roi rejected the design for unknown reasons.

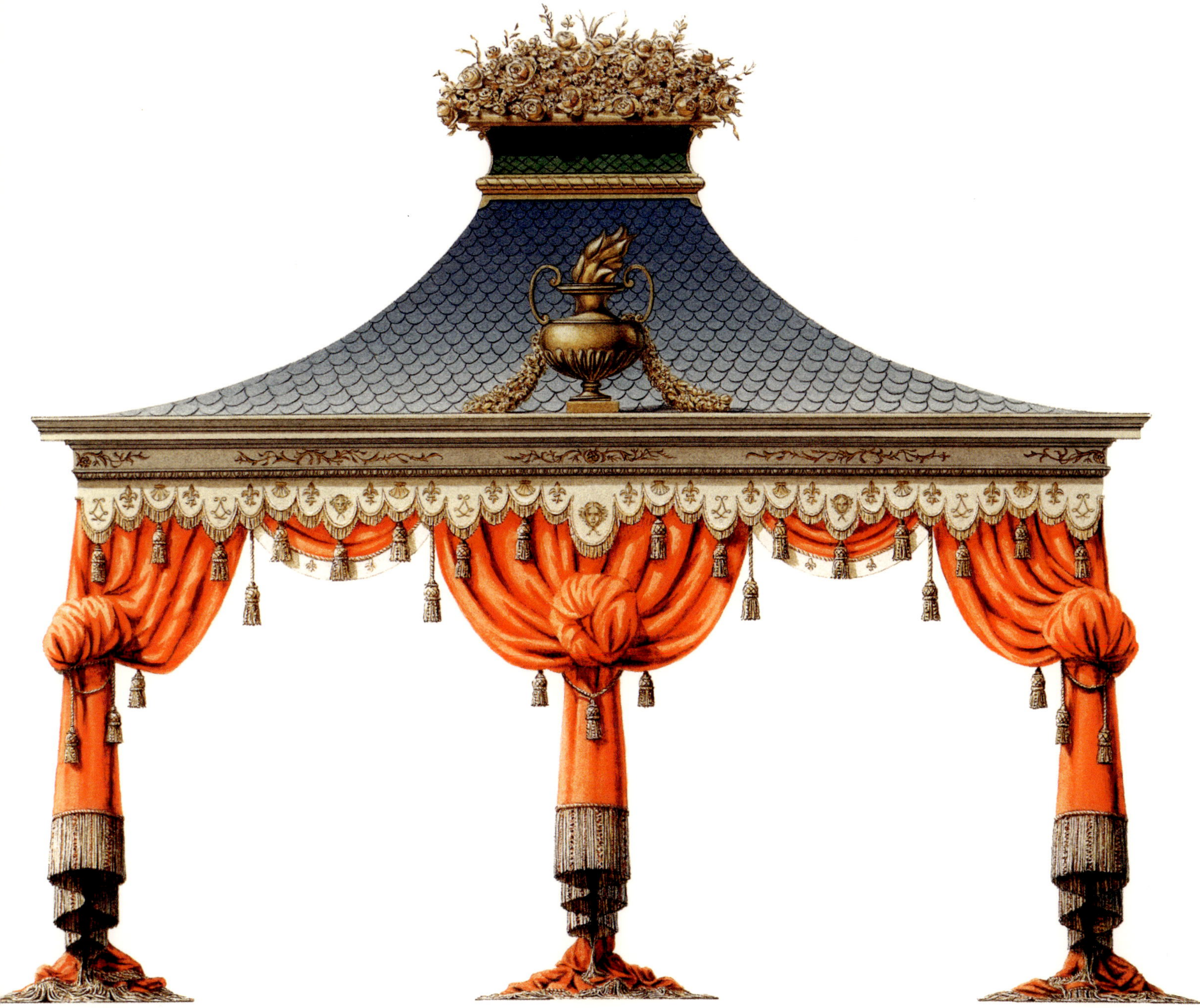

Chinese House at Armainvilliers

Duc de Penthièvre, commissioner
Jean-Augustin Renard, architect
built circa 1780
destroyed

THIS PAVILION perfectly illustrates the influence of Sir William Chambers' publications, being a virtual copy of plate II of his *Design of Chinese Buildings,* published in 1757. The architect of record is Jean-Augustin Renard (1744–1807), building for the Duc de Penthièvre, distant cousin to Louis XVI and inheritor of much of Sun King's largesse to his illegitimate offspring. Unburdened by the de facto bankruptcy of the state that afflicted the king, the duke was the richest man in France, a pious widower who took pleasure in indulging his sheltered and sentimental daughter-in-law, the Princesse de Lamballe. The construction of extensive folly gardens at Rambouillet and Armainvilliers, two of his numerous estates, was undertaken to divert her, and the numerous pagodas Renard designed (*pp. 113, 115*) indicate that Chinoiserie was her favored architectural style.

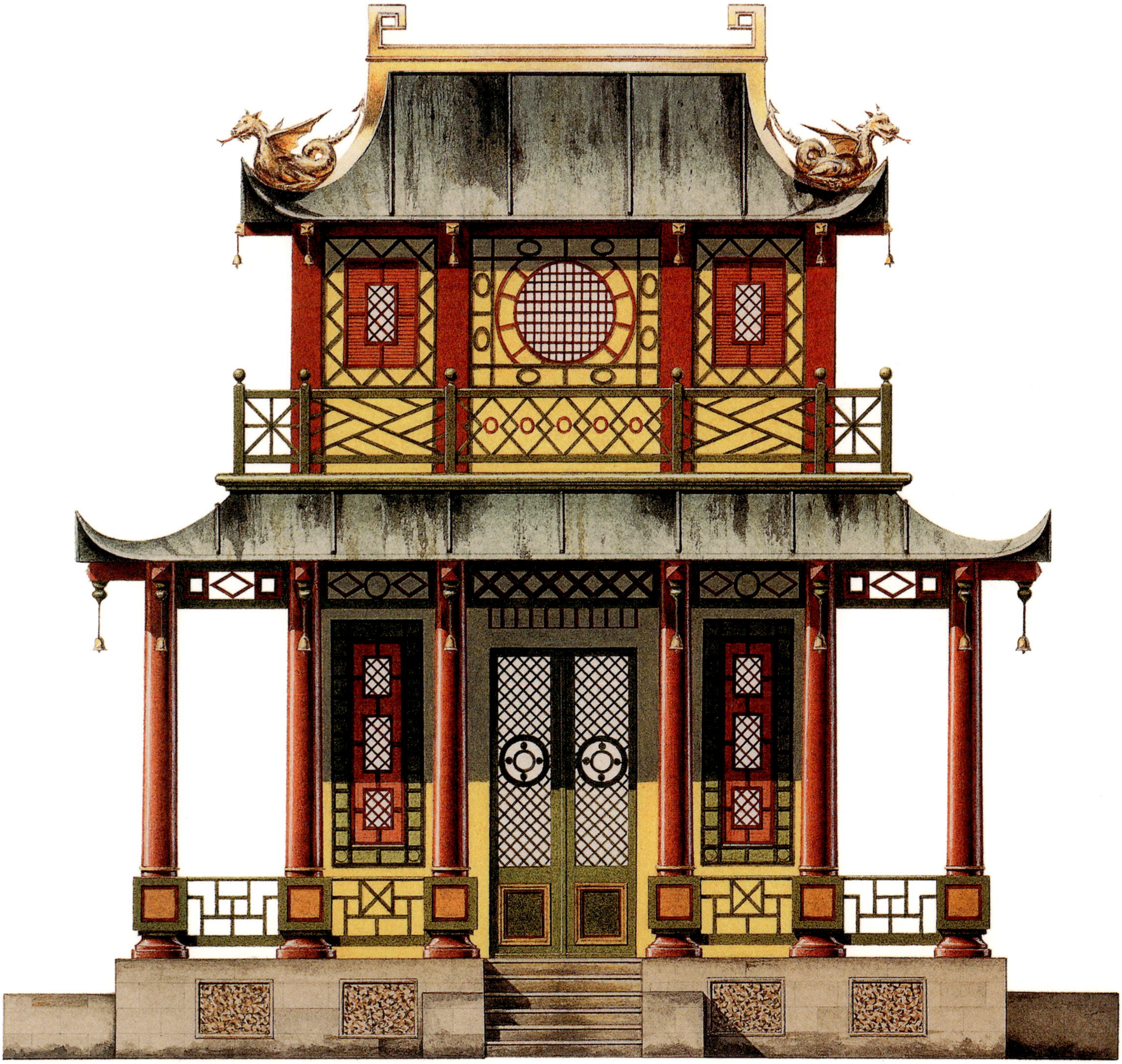

PAGODA AT ARMAINVILLIERS

Duc de Penthièvre, commissioner
Jean-Augustin Renard, architect
built circa 1780
destroyed

Armainvilliers was an unusually large estate to the southeast of Paris, with an extensive hunting park and an Anglo-Chinese garden constructed under the supervision of the architect Jean-Augustin Renard. This sober, hexagonally planned pagoda, along with the Chinese House (*preceding page*), were part of an ensemble of follies that included the Turkish Pavilion, a large domed mosque flanked by minarets probably inspired by Sir William Chambers' design for Kew, and the Gothic Tower, a turreted bathing pavilion set astride an arched grotto. Though representing widely divergent cultures and architectural styles, both follies shared the same construction materials as this pagoda—bands of brick alternating with tufa or limestone. By subordinating each individual design to an aesthetic norm, Renard found an effective means to permit souvenirs of Islam, medieval Europe and China to stand side by side in relative harmony. The pagoda features an abstracted moon gate, circular openings that are symbolic of good fortune.

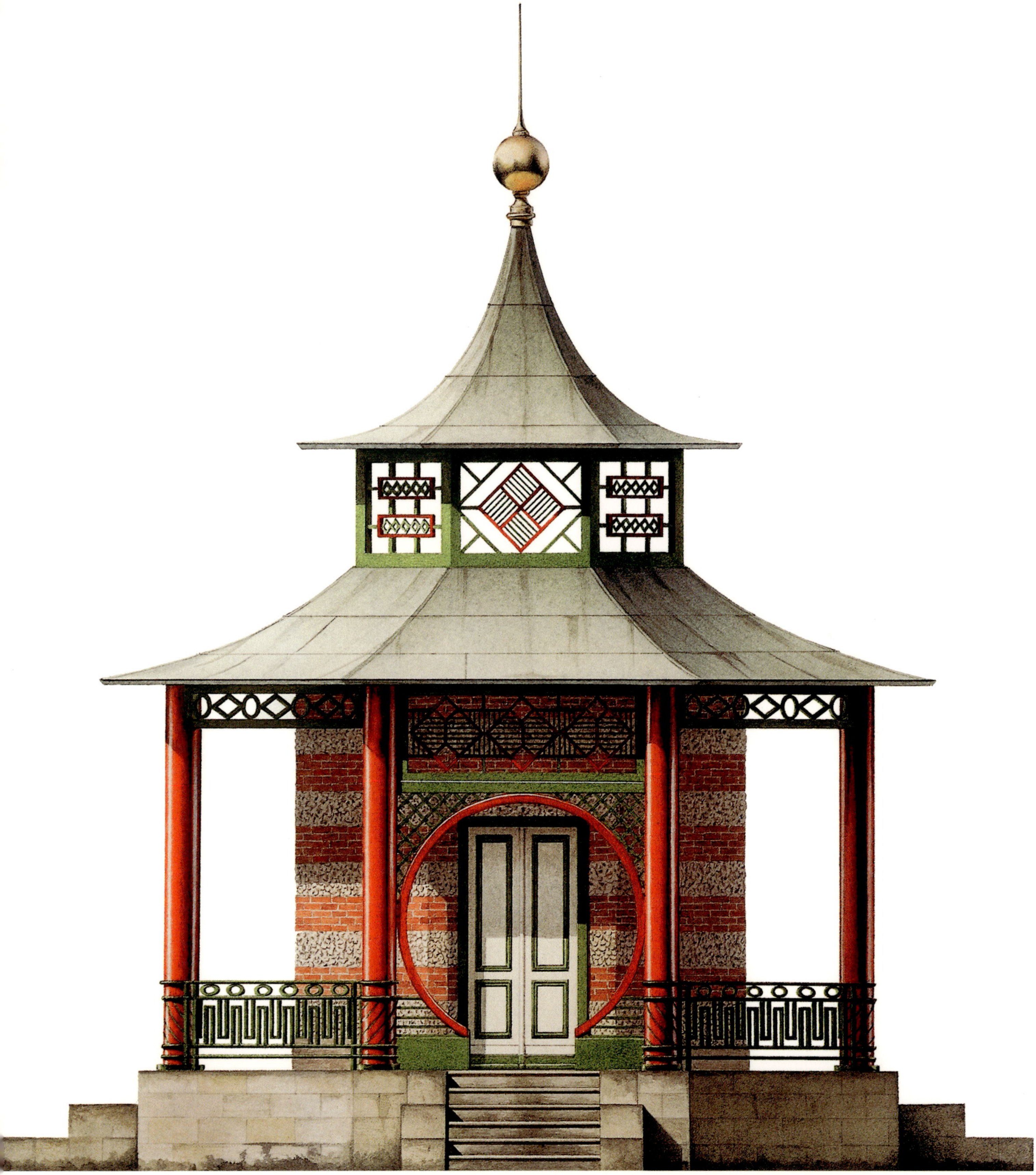

Pagoda at Rambouillet

Duc de Penthièvre, commissioner
attributed to architect Jean-Augustin Renard
built circa 1780
destroyed

The pagoda at Rambouillet was commissioned by the Duc de Penthièvre before 1784, as a part of the great park's transformation into an English-style landscape garden, and was probably built for the amusement of his widowed daughter-in-law, the Princesse de Lamballe. The pagoda straddled a rockwork grotto that still divides a watercourse, and its access stairs served as the bridge for a major garden path. It was a simple frame structure with large wooden panels that could be propped open to admit light and air, and the dragons mounted on the corners of the roof were a free interpretation of traditional Chinese decorations—as was the crowning *chattra*, a series of graded hoops with bells—testifying to a desire for greater authenticity in later Chinoiserie follies.

The architect remains anonymous, but was probably the Inspector of the King's Buildings, Jean-Augustin Renard, architect also of the garden follies at Armainvilliers, another of the Duke's numerous estates. Renard masterfully employs three picturesque elements key to creating a successful Chinoiserie structure: rocks, water and bright colors evoking the spirit of the Orient.

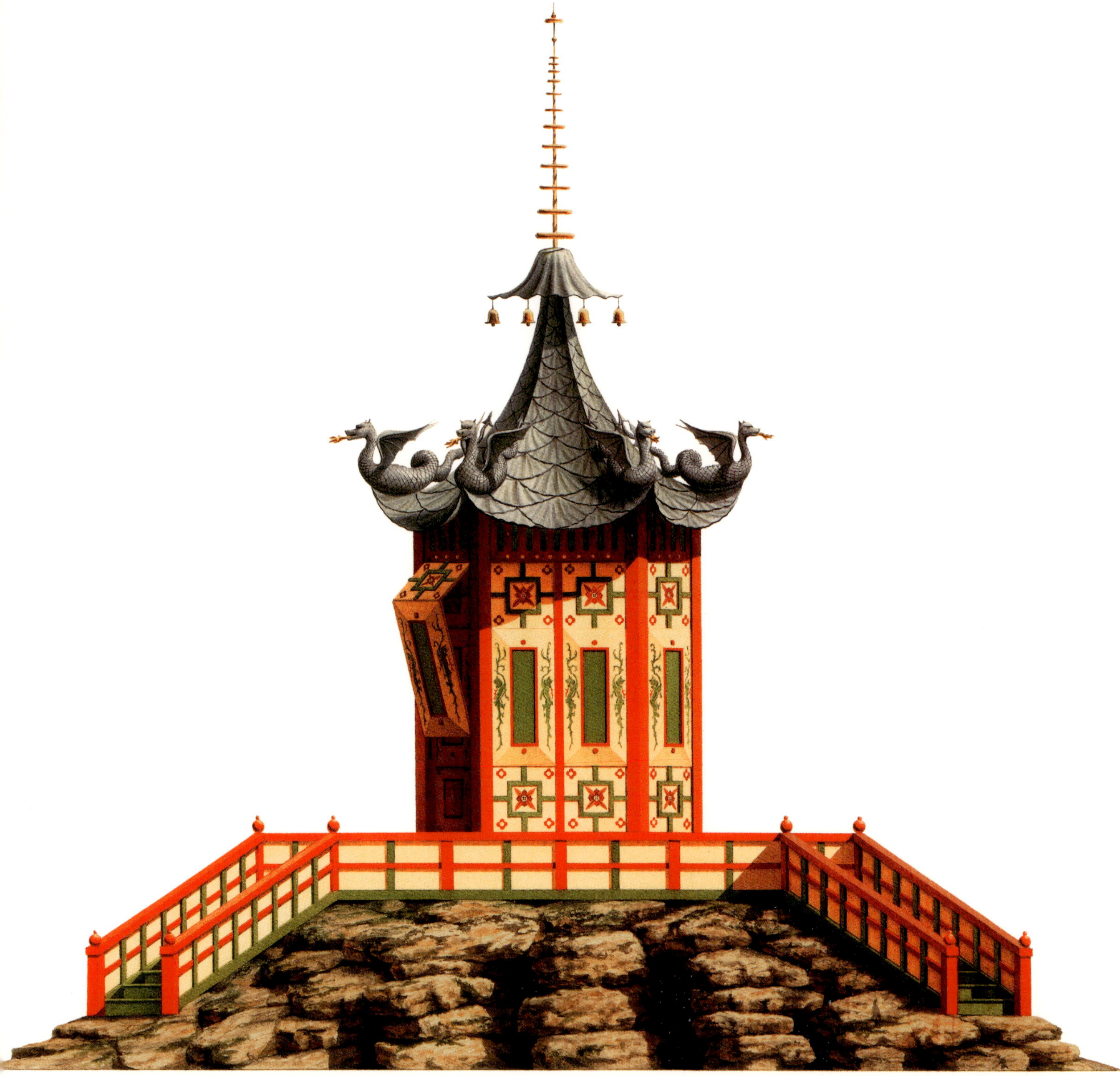

Dovecote for Attichy

Duchesse de la Tremoïlle, commissioner
Francesco Bettini, architect
designed circa 1780
unbuilt project

Francesco bettini, the Italian architect who drew this remarkable dovecote for the gardens of the Duchesse de la Tremoïlle at Attichy, was also a festival designer, decorator and pupil of the engraver Georges Le Rouge, who called him "full of genius." Bettini spent ten years in Paris, leaving in 1784, and provided a number of plates for Le Rouge's monumental collection, *Les Jardins Anglo-Chinois à la Mode,* including this design, which figures twice in the compilation, later recycled for another garden near Paris proposed for a nameless count.

He also engraved the plate featuring the Pagoda at Rambouillet (*p. 134*) for Le Rouge, which clearly provided much of his inspiration—along with Sir William Chambers' inevitable pagoda at Kew gardens—for the dovecote's design. The circular openings of the small ground-floor salon, also seen at the pagoda at Armainvilliers (*p. 113*), were architectural citations of symbolically charged Chinese moon gates, and were to be closed by curtains to offer a moment of repose during a promenade.

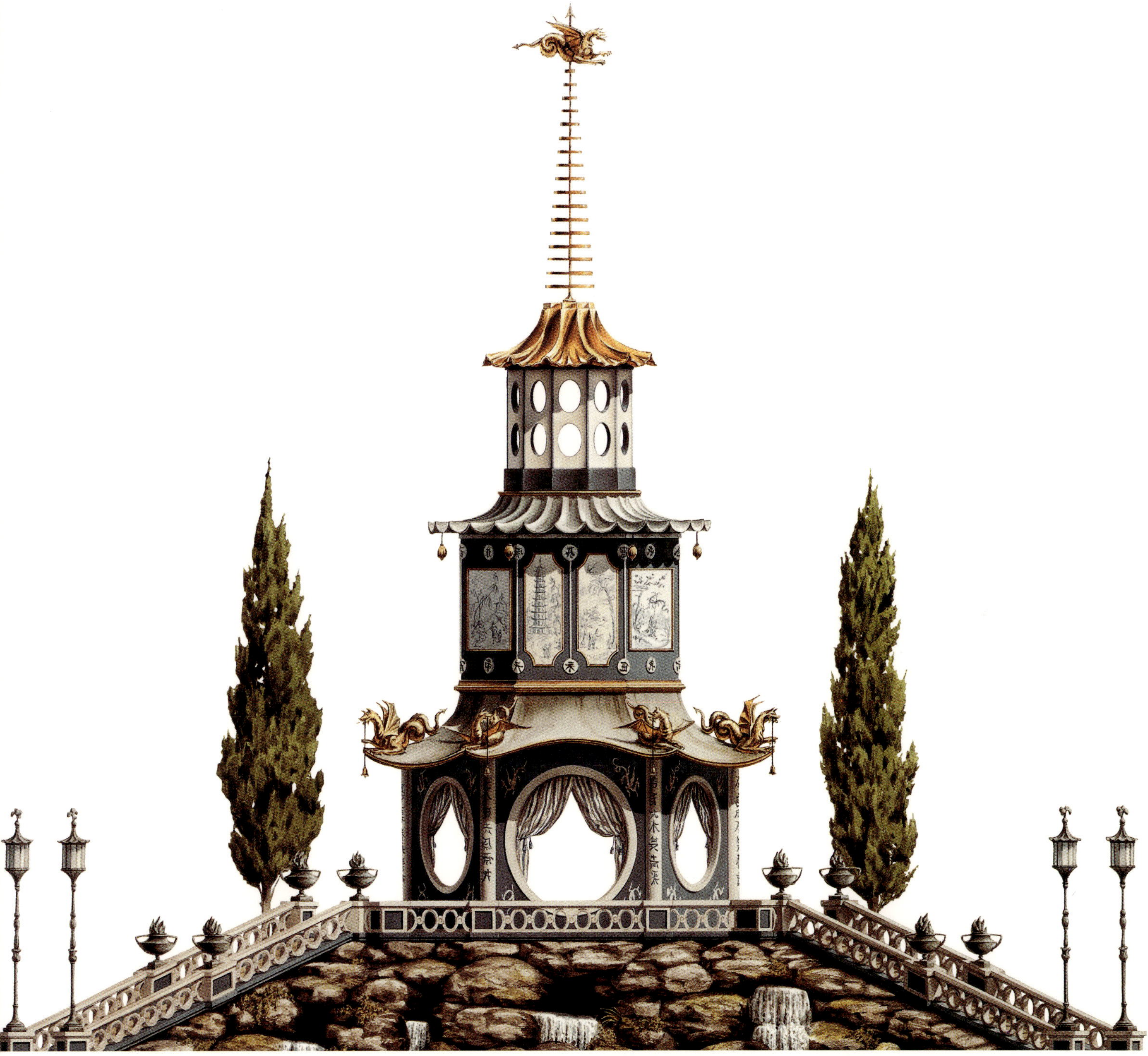

*Neither grandeur nor rich materials distinguish Chinese edifices,
but there is a singularity in their manner, a rightness in their proportion,
a simplicity, sometimes even a beauty in their form, that merits our attention.*

Sir William Chambers

The iconic porcelain tower at Nanking, engraved by Athanasius Kirchner after Nieuhoff.

The PORCELANE TOWER *at* NAN-KING *from* Nieuhof

Pagoda at Bonnelles

Duc d'Uzès, commissioner
Francesco Bettini, architect
designed circa 1780
unbuilt project

A COUNTRY ESTATE ringed by a canal and bisected by a vast cross axis cut through a hunting wood, Bonnelles was laid out in the classical tradition of Le Nôtre, but with orchards and kitchen gardens substituted for the formal parterres usually surrounding the château. This winsome pagoda was part of an extensive ensemble of a lake, grotto, bridges and pavilions—in essence an Anglo-Chinese folly garden in miniature. The pagoda-belvedere stood atop a large artificial rockwork dominating the lake and was reached by a series of rustic, arching footbridges, the last of which sprung from a small island featuring the Philosopher's Pavilion, a tiny, thatch-roofed hermit's hut (*p. 135*).

The pagoda, square in plan and with large circular windows, featured detached corner columns inscribed with fanciful Chinese inscriptions. These same elements are found in various designs drawn by the Italian architect and festival designer Francesco Bettini—among them the project for a pagoda at Attichy for the Duchesse d'Uzès' sister, the Duchesse de la Tremoïlle (*p. 117*)—strongly suggesting that Bettini authored the pagoda at Bonnelles as well.

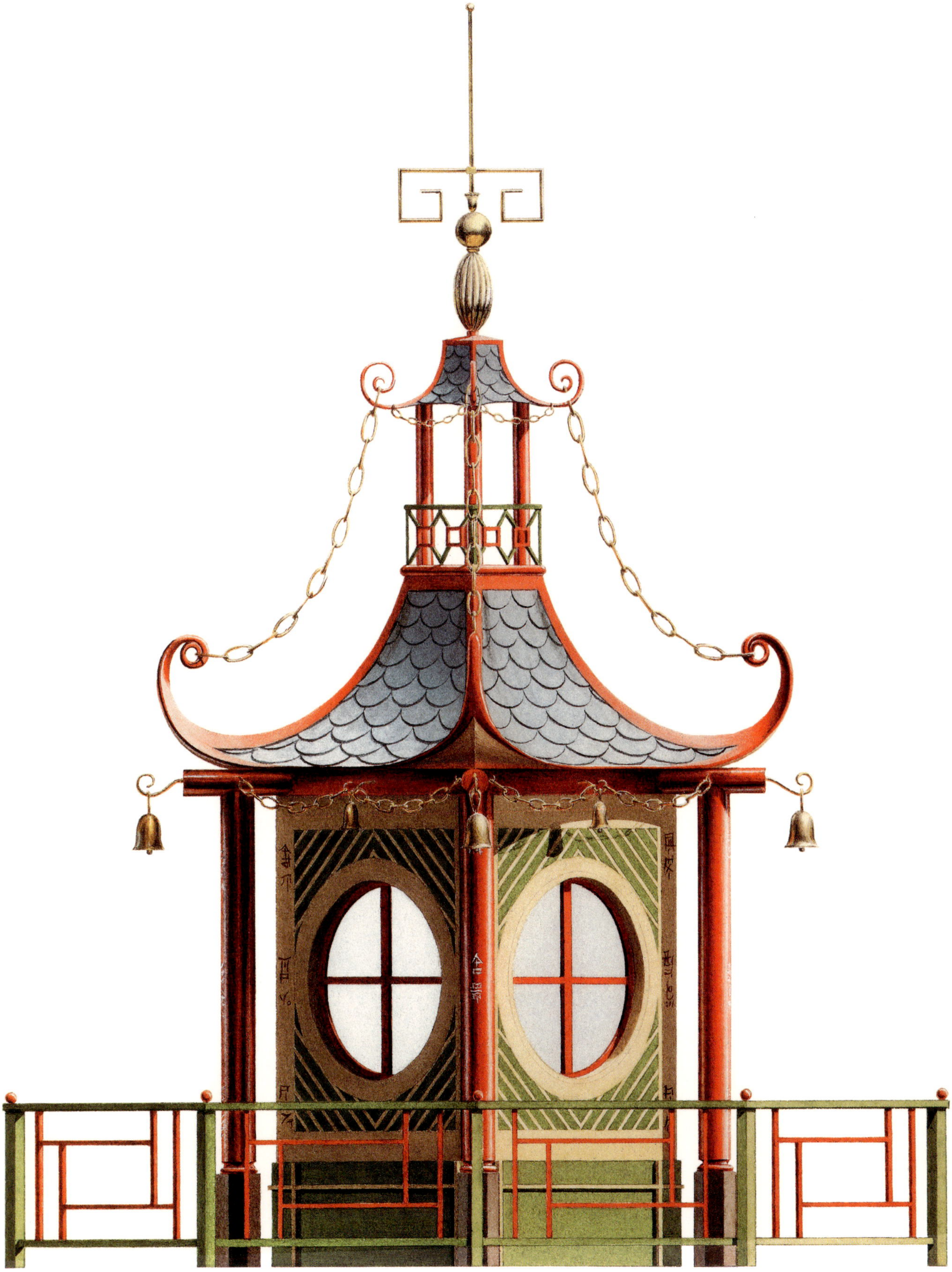

Chinese Pavilion at Romainville

Marquis de Ségur, commissioner
Baron de Besenval, architect
built circa 1780
destroyed

Romainville, a sober country château overlooking a simple landscape park, was the property of the Marquis de Ségur, Minister of War under Louis XVI. His wife's lover was the Baron de Besenval, the prototype of the avid amateur aristocrat-architect—a polished courtier, intimate of Marie-Antoinette, whom Sainte-Beuve called "the most French Swiss that there ever was." In an arrangement that was typically ancien régime, the Marquis, mindful of Besenval's intimacy with the queen, invited his wife's lover and the true father of his heir to oversee the transformation of his estate.

Inspired by Richard Mique's work for the queen at Trianon, Besenval designed three follies for the park of Romainville: the Roman Temple, a Corinthian rotunda based on the Temple of Love; the Octagonal Pavilion, reprising the queen's Belvedere; and the Chinese Pavilion, which apparently was his own original design. Sited on sloping land near the château's terrace and terminating a watercourse, the pagoda featured an unusual hexagonal footprint and stood on a circular stone plinth. Small, abrupt earthen mounds, nearly as tall as the pagoda itself, rose nearby, bracketing the view toward the prairie below. Though Romainville has been destroyed, copies of the Chinese Pavilion stand in the gardens of Cliveden, England, and at Bagatelle.

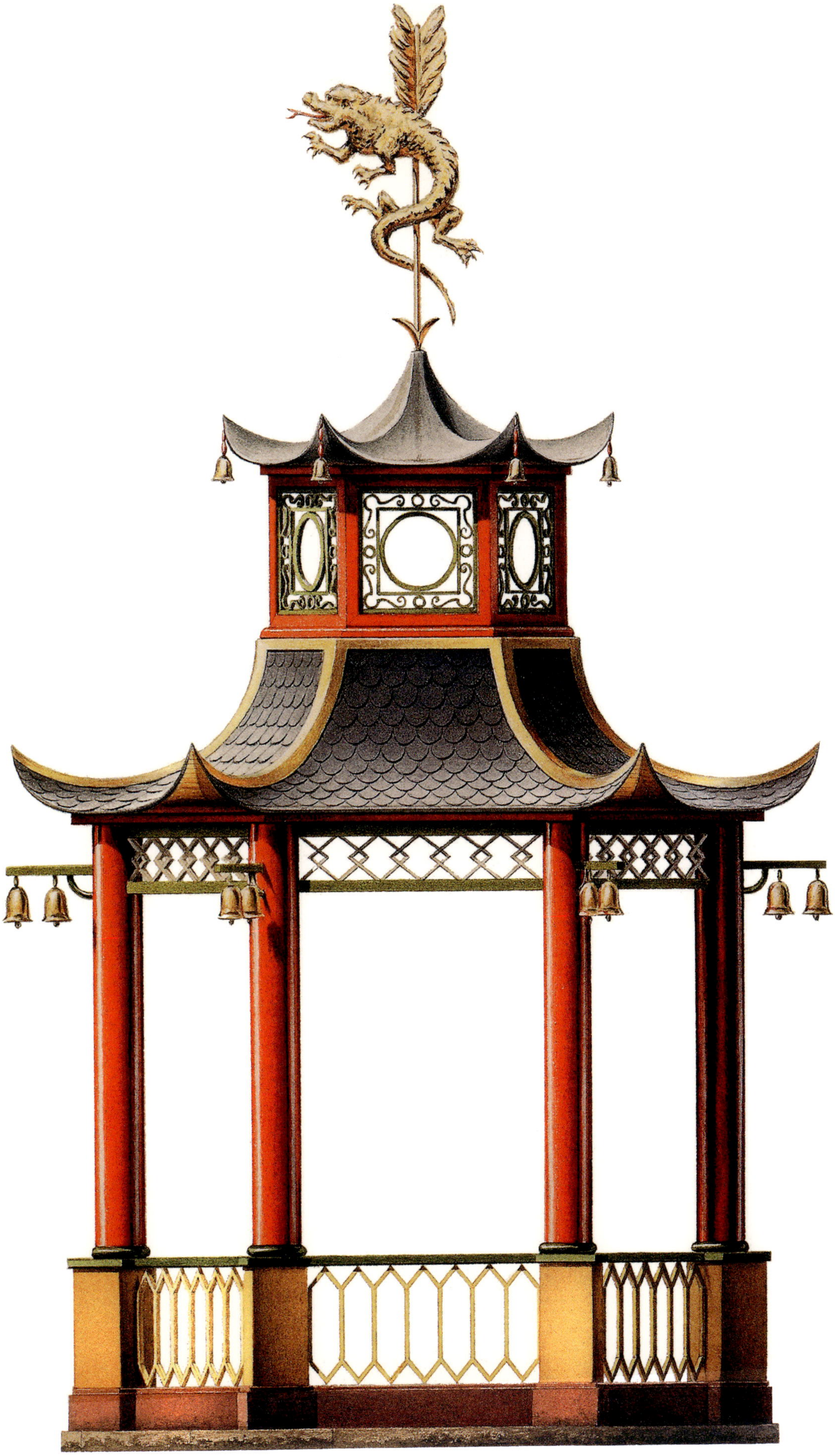

Chinese Pavilion at Stors

Prince de Conti, commissioner
anonymous architect
built circa 1780
extant

Even in its present state of suspended dilapidation, Stors exudes an atmosphere of tranquility and refinement certain to a few small manors nestled about the open countryside of the Île-de-France. The handsome Régence residence is set at the base of a low ridge overlooking the river Oise, its intimate scale midway between that of manor and château. In 1756 the Prince de Conti purchased the estate to lodge guests of the nearby Château de l'Isle-Adam, from which he oversaw the numerous Conti properties in the region.

The great surprise of the garden, shifting the scale of the estate from intimacy to grandeur, is extensive limestone terracing, rising in three tiers on the hillside facing the château. The lowest level, a pediment-shaped retaining wall, arcs to embrace a large oval basin, forming a grand *fer-à-cheval* earthen ramp rising to a limestone terrace well over sixty yards long.

Paired stone pagodas were erected above the corner buttresses terminating this terrace—miniature Oriental belvederes but nine feet to a side. Behind rises a high, arcaded retaining wall crowned by a classical balustrade, offering extensive views over the surrounding countryside. The pagodas' severe, faceted stonework piers share the austere linearity of the upper terraces, but are offset by playful roofs and the delicate filigree of their wooden screens.

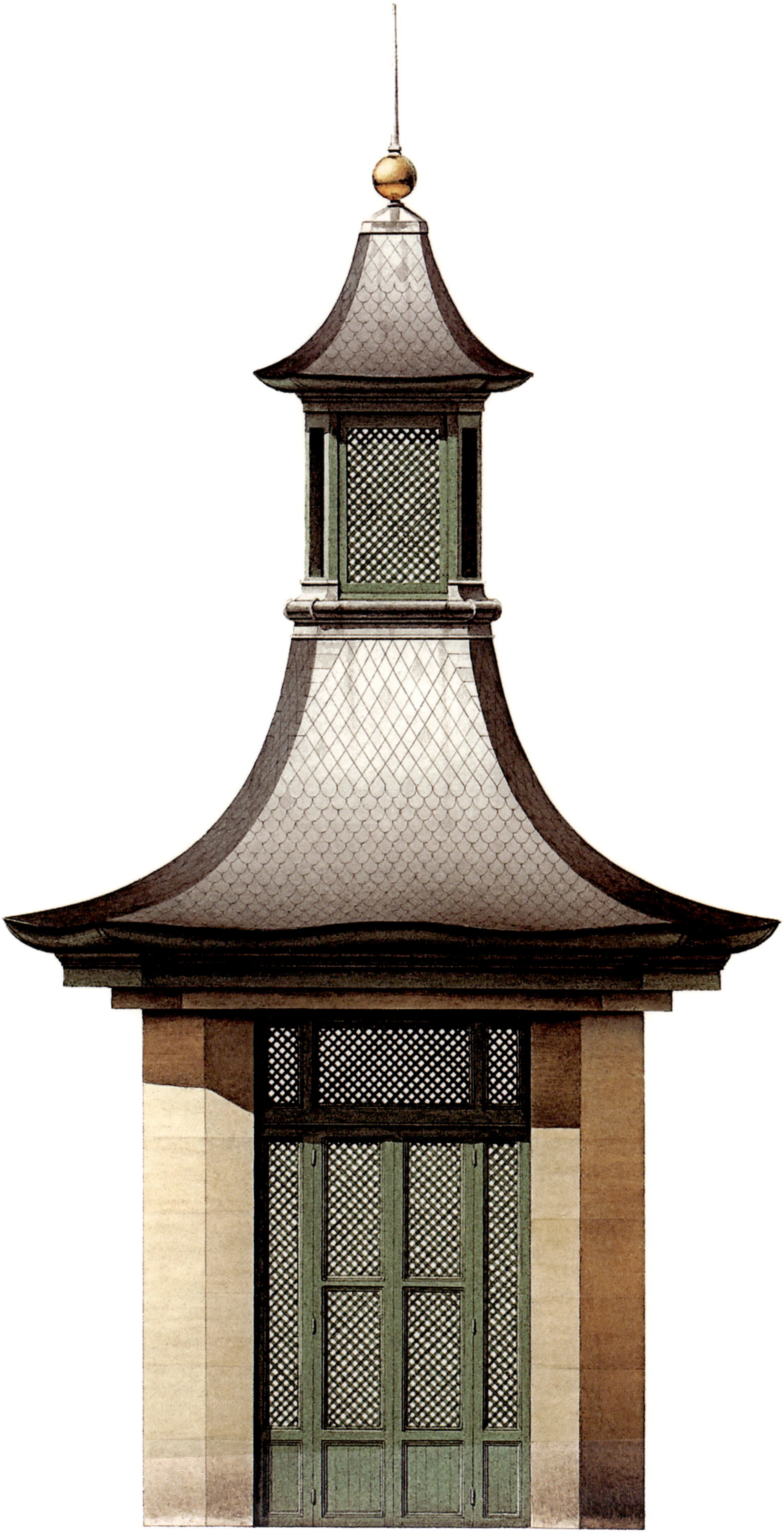

Chinese Tent for Trianon Versailles

Marie-Antoinette, commissioner
Jean-Baptiste Pillement, architect
designed 1780
unbuilt project

Sketched by an unknown draftsman in the atelier of Jean-Baptiste Pillement, the foremost decorative painter of his time, this project for a tented bench set in a niched wall is believed to be one of the many unrealized projects conceived to embellish Marie-Antoinette's gardens at Trianon. The diminutive folly, a simple wooden structure covered with painted canvas and decorated with ostrich plumes, encapsulates the enchanting spirit of French Chinoiserie, ingeniously mixing disparate styles and decorative elements to achieve a picturesque tour de force. As with the numerous temporary tents *à la turc* or *à la chinoise* erected for the queen's lavish garden fêtes at Trianon, the tent's ancestors are the sumptuous tents erected for the *divertissements* of Louis XIV in the gardens of Versailles.

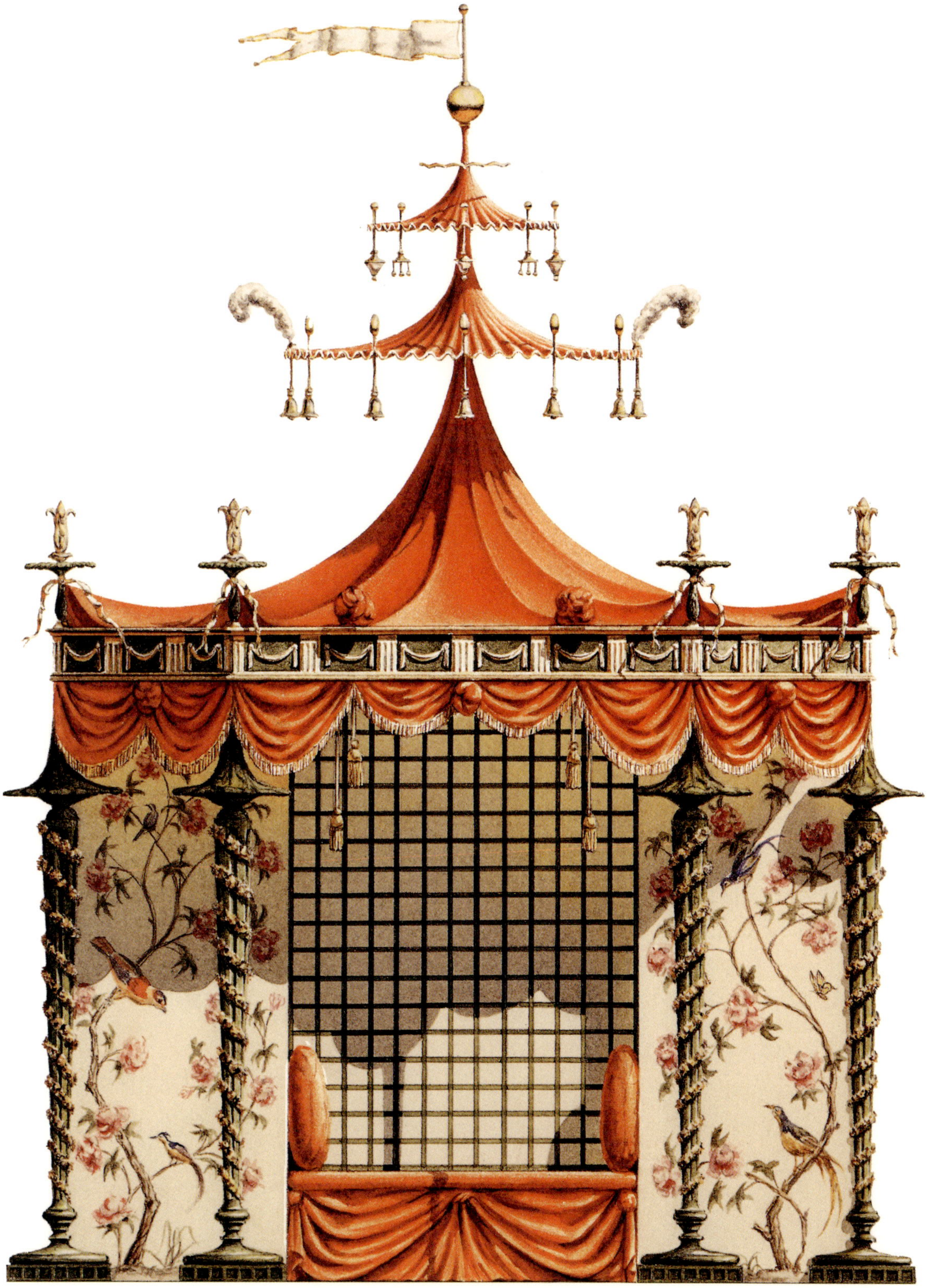

Oriental Kiosk at Betz

Princesse de Monaco, commissioner
Duc d'Harcourt and Hubert Robert, architects
built circa 1784
destroyed

The estate of Betz was the gift of the Prince de Condé, owner of nearby Chantilly, to his declared mistress, the Princesse de Monaco. Under the supervision of the Duc d'Harcourt, an avid amateur gardener and architect, and Hubert Robert, painter of architectural ruins without equal and gardener to Louis XVI, the princess became an impassioned builder and directed the creation of an extensive *anglo-chinois* folly garden in the last years before the Revolution. Like so many other gardens of the period, Betz became a curio cabinet of follies, with more than a dozen major structures skillfully wedged into a few walled hectares, including not simply a sarcophagus, as at Ermenonville, but an entire Valley of Tombs, as well as an obelisk commemorating American independence.

The pagoda was a spirited, completely Western confection, employing the stock repertoire of Chinoiserie motifs with assurance and panache. Its solid, cylindrical core, foreign to Chinese precedents, was doubtless inspired by the Chinese Kiosk at Chantilly, built in 1771 for the princess's lover, and among the earliest Chinoiseries in France. A Chinese Bridge, its pendant, competed with a Druid's Temple, the neoclassical Temple of Friendship (still extant) and a grandiose feudal ruin authored by Robert. The estate remains intact but lacks both its original château and most of its follies.

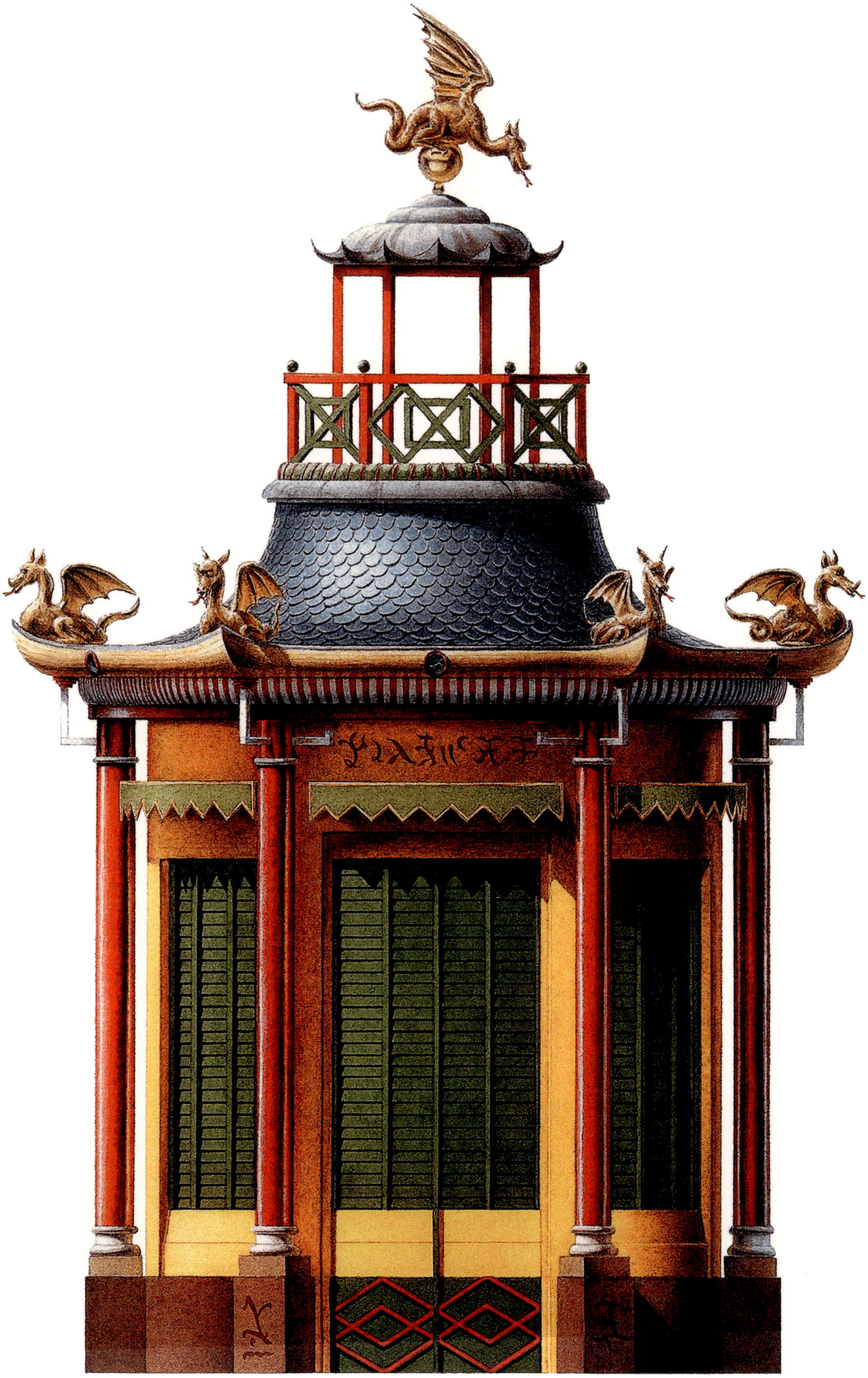

Georges Le Rouge

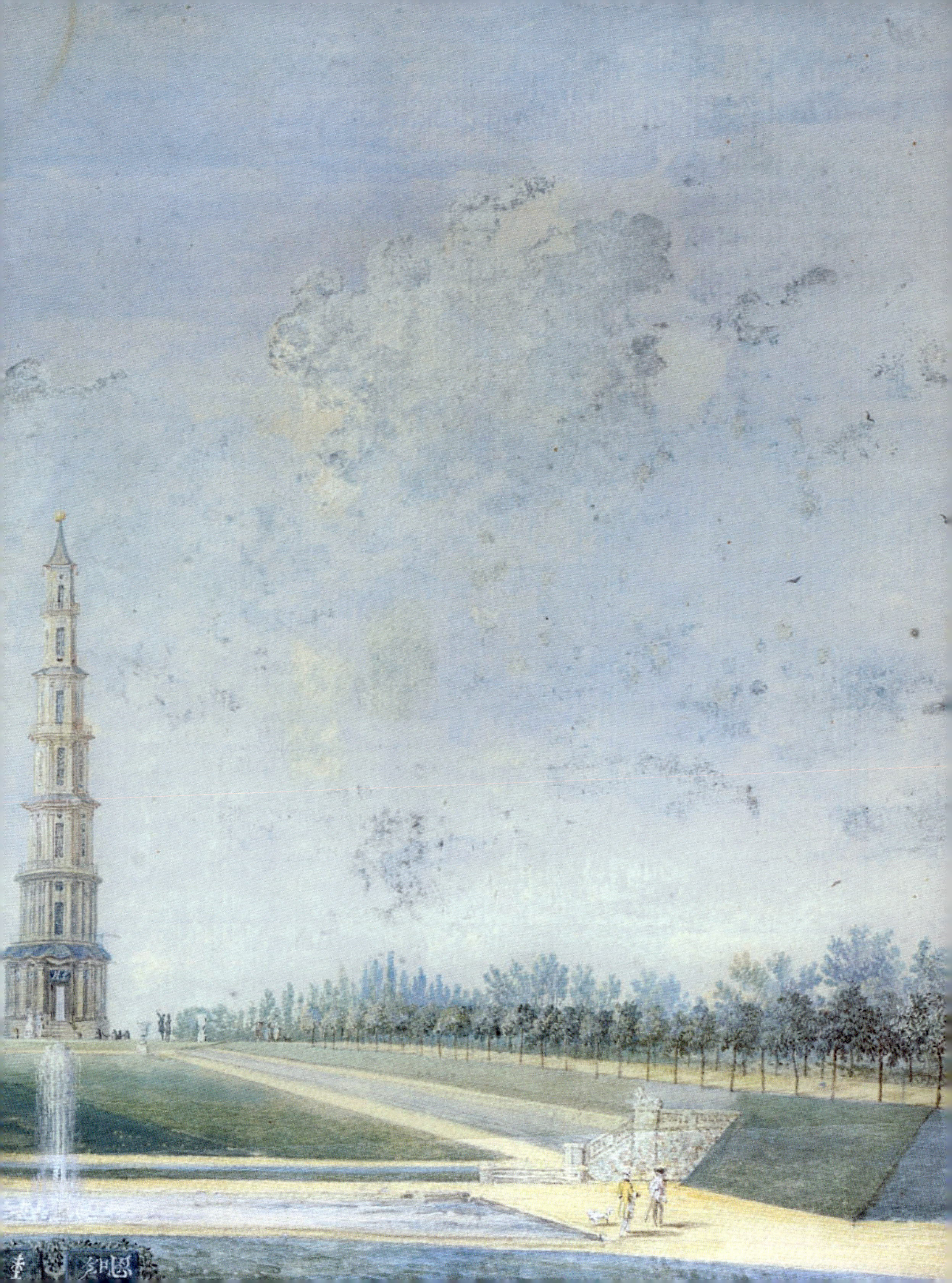

Previous pages: The Pagoda at Chanteloup, *a gouache miniature by Nicolas von Blarenberghe.*

Georges Le Rouge

If Sir William Chambers was the begetter of the last and most passionate chapter of the Chinoiserie craze in Europe, then Georges Le Rouge must be considered its chronicler. Born in Hanover at the outset of the eighteenth century, Le Rouge was in all probability the son of the French architect Louis Remy de la Fosse, though he remained purposefully vague about his origins throughout his life. His wandering years took him across the German principalities to England, where he pursued studies as an engineer, land surveyor and geographer. Named cartographer to Louis XV, Le Rouge settled in Paris in 1736 and attached himself to the household of the Maréchal Maurice de Saxe, who named him a lieutenant of his regiment, an honorific that eased access to the higher echelons of society, though his ascent was but a shadow of Chambers' astonishing rise.

In 1741 Le Rouge opened a shop dedicated to almanacs and engravings, specializing in military maps and atlases. He also offered a wide array of printed materials such as views of Parisian monuments, and imported engravings from England and Germany, which kept him abreast of the latest European developments in architecture and gardening. Though his hope of becoming an eminent architect was never realized, Le Rouge moved freely in the architectural milieu of the capitol: several of the era's foremost architects were friends and clients, and often furnished designs of executed and unexecuted projects to distribute as engravings.

The incarnation of the eighteenth century's jack-of-all-trades, Le Rouge would be today forgotten but for a fortuitous encounter with Chambers in Paris in 1774. His business engraving and distributing military maps had stagnated with the long peace following the Seven Years' War, and the outbreak of the War of American Independence was to offer only the slightest of respites. Chambers, who had recently

Chinoiseries

The Pagoda at Rambouillet (p. 115), *astride a rockwork cascade, from Le Rouge.*

published his *Dissertation*, advised Le Rouge that the mounting fascination with gardening was a lucrative means to revive his failing publishing venture.

The vanguard French theorists Duchesne, Watelet and Morel had all published treatises between 1771 and 1776, and it was at this juncture that Le Rouge began his monumental compilation of engravings documenting the latest trends in European landscape gardens, *Les Jardins Anglo-Chinois à la Mode*. Its twenty-one albums, released intermittently over a fifteen-year period, illustrated Europe's most famous and outlandish gardens and garden structures, and his compendium

Georges Le Rouge

The Pagoda at Bonnelles (p. 121), astraddle its grotto, from Le Rouge.

would become the prime visual reference consulted by those laying out an Anglo-Chinese garden. Its cumulative influence was rivaled only by Chambers' own publications, and it was Le Rouge himself who coined the term *anglo-chinois* in one of his first albums.

Le Rouge followed no discernible publishing plan and printed whatever came to hand, shamelessly plagiarizing older engravings and plans dating back two decades and more—but such lapses were the inevitable result of his struggle for solvency. Nonetheless, his plates are the only surviving documentation of numerous European parks and gardens that otherwise would have fallen into oblivion. The Bagno, the Prince of Steinfurt's cluttered Vauxhall garden in Westfalia, is typical among them. Based on French models, the folly garden

Chinoiseries

at Steinfurt was scattered with replicas taken from Le Rouge's pages, including his Chinese tents (*pp. 89, 91*) and the Chinese House at the Désert de Retz (*p. 75*). The Bagno gardens appeared in the last album Le Rouge published, only months after the outbreak of the French Revolution, which ended the world he had so diligently chronicled.

While apparently no pavilion, garden bridge or folly escaped him, Le Rouge never insisted on factual authenticity, and sheer quantity often substituted for accuracy and originality. Nonetheless, the breadth of his undertaking was truly unprecedented.

Like their predecessors, who derived their knowledge of the Celestial Empire from the nebulous accounts of travelers and merchants, Le Rouge's audience accepted his engravings as an inspiration and a point of departure often as removed from reality as the Jesuit depictions of China in the preceding century. The *jardin anglo-chinois* was a conscious deception, though a spirited one, whose inner logic Julie in *La Nouvelle Héloïse* had cleverly anticipated: "It is true that nature did everything, but under my command, and there is nothing I did not order."

Georges Le Rouge

"One cannot lay out a garden without a little poetry," Jean-François Bélanger remarked, and Le Rouge presented a naïve verity easily grasped by the public. With an endearing and often alarming *horror vacui*, he seemed compelled to embellish his work, adding scenes in the blank corners of plans—a view of Frederick the Great's Neues Palais is found floating in a demi-lune basin at Marly—editing and rearranging until his engravings achieved an equilibrium of density only he could fathom. In consequence the plates are nearly as suspect as they are instructive and can be considered only a starting point for research on any particular garden or building, but nonetheless the entirety of the twenty-one albums is unsurpassed for its wealth of information.

His publication of two late albums depicting actual Chinese gardens was a major achievement but had no measurable impact on the development of the Anglo-Chinese garden, since by the 1780s Europeans already believed they understood them, and so the true merit of Le Rouge's compilation rests in its depiction of a lost world, as a testament to generations who sought arcadia in the vision of Cathay.

Opposite: The Pagoda at Kew Gardens by Sir William Chambers (pp. 92-93), *published by Le Rouge in his eleventh album. Inspired by the porcelain tower at Nanking, the famed tower in turn inspired the Pagoda at Chanteloup.*

Lake Pagoda at Folie Sainte-James

Baron Sainte-James, commissioner
François-Joseph Bélanger, architect
built circa 1784
destroyed

Claude Baudard, Baron de Sainte-Gemmes, son of a wealthy tax collector, was a fervent anglophile who took the name Sainte-James and occupied his free time with monumental social ambitions. In 1772 he purchased land in Neuilly near Bagatelle and soon conceived a scheme to eclipse the Comte d'Artois and his estate, and in 1781 offered Bagatelle's architect, François-Joseph Bélanger, free reign to "Build whatever you like, provided it is expensive." Artois, not amused by this brazen upstart, quietly ordered Bélanger, who remained in his employ, to "ruin Sainte-James," a mission the architect accepted with relish. The result was a surprisingly intimate residence, little more than an excuse for an extensive folly park that would absorb much of Sainte-James' fortune and tax the limits of Bélanger's creative energies.

Apart from a massive grotto sheltering a Greek temple portico, dubbed "the eighth wonder of the world" by contemporaries, the Lake Pagoda was the estate's most picturesque folly. The foursquare latticework structure stood on pylons in an artificial lake and was reached by a Chinese skiff with its own fretwork pagoda canopy. The color scheme presented here is one of the few to have been transmitted from the period, found on a period engraving, though it is impossible to determine whether it is a valid representation or the colorist's fanciful interpretation.

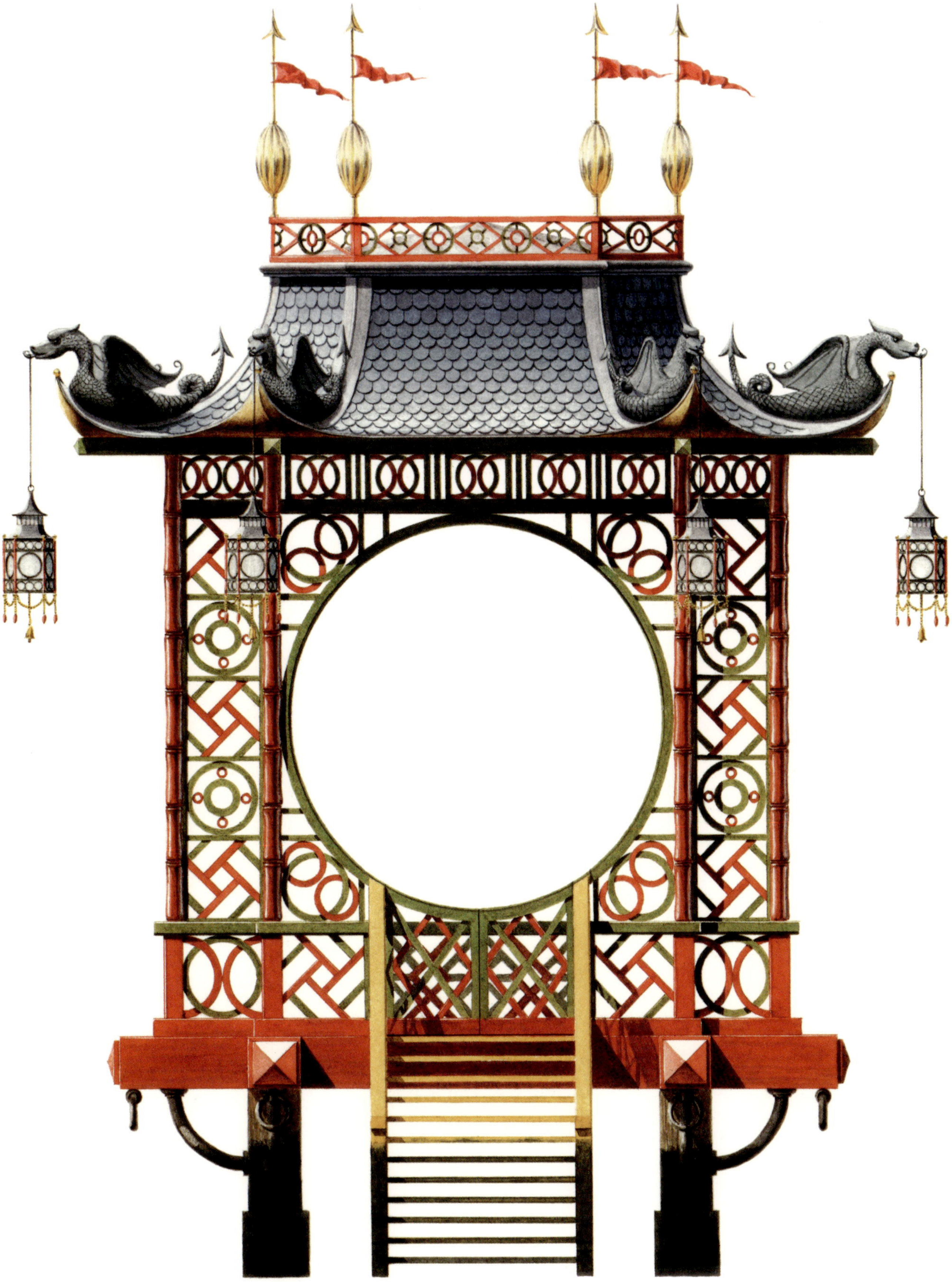

Gothic Monument at Folie Sainte-James

Baron Sainte-James, commissioner
François-Joseph Bélanger, architect
built circa 1784
destroyed

Like the Baron Sainte-James himself, his singular folly garden at Neuilly consisted of equal measures of vainglory and excess—a place of superlatives and extremes where the rage for the picturesque most nearly approached parody and madness. Jean-Charles Krafft, who catalogued the era's garden architecture, proffered a revealing description of the Folie Sainte-James' seventeen hermetic acres: "This grand garden is divided into meadows, groves, orchards, vineyards, vegetable gardens, beds for exotic plants, arbors, flowerbeds, bosquets, lawns, fields, etc.…their variety provides alternating views of mountains and valleys, hills and plains…the walks are so myriad that one easily loses oneself and is unable to find one's way out of the compound."

Eclectically furnished, the garden contained follies created as elements of a rich, colorful and fantastic ensemble, and their intended effects owed more to the mannered theatricality of contemporary comedies than to the lofty precepts of the French architectural tradition. The Gothic Monument is a perfect exemplar of this stylistic disorder—a playful admixture of Moorish, Gothic and Renaissance elements, its sloped roof the only trace in its mongrel design of a Chinoiserie heritage. The elaborately decorated eye-catcher, triangular in plan, served ostensibly as little more than a shaded garden bench.

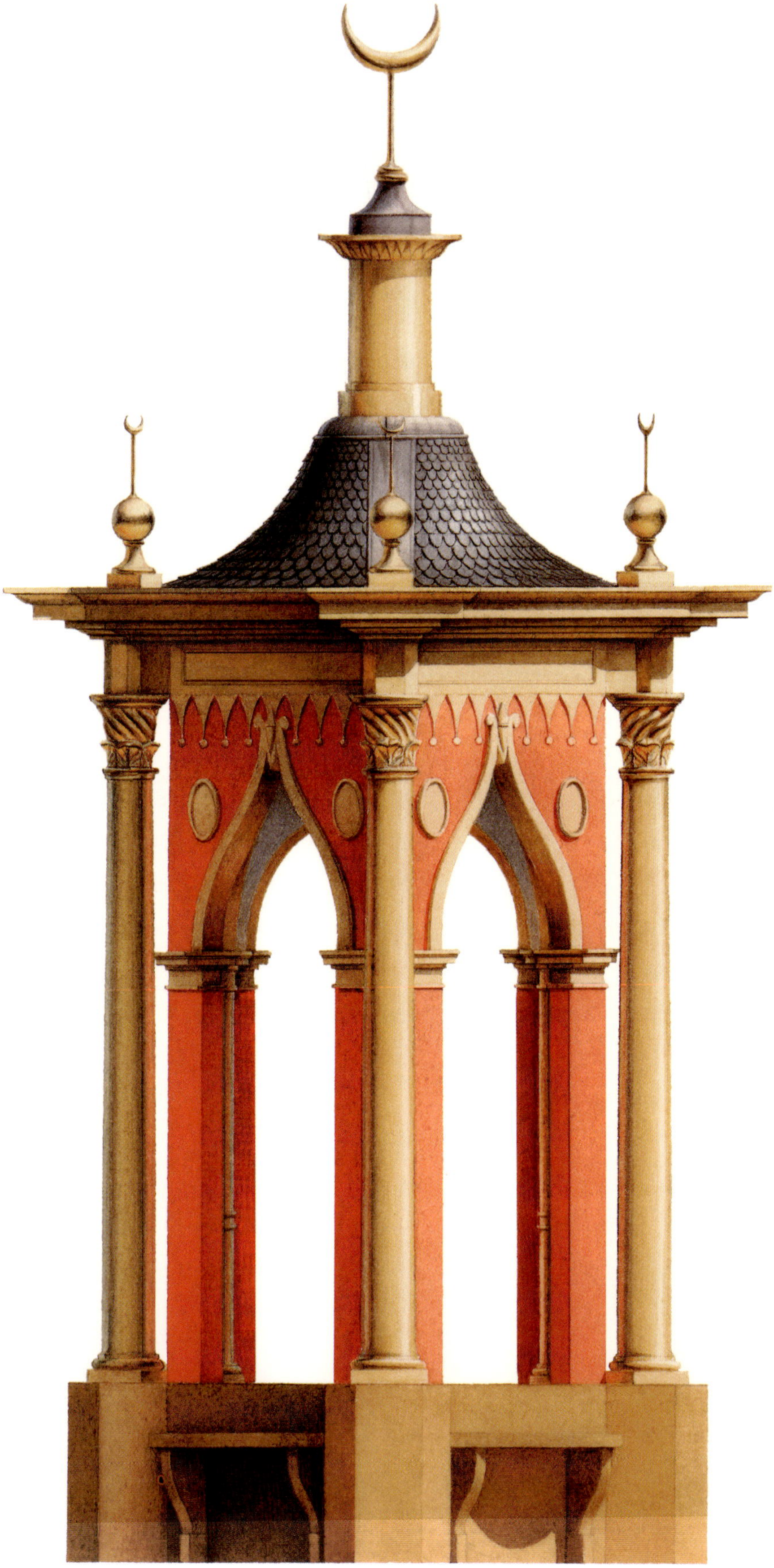

Chinese Bridge at Laxenburg

Emperor Joseph II, commissioner
Februe d'Archenbault, architect
built circa 1785
destroyed

The imperial estate of Laxenburg was a Hapsburg retreat in the countryside near Vienna with an English landscape park laid out for Joseph II by the military engineer Februe d'Archenbault in 1782. The Chinese Bridge was a masterpiece of theatrical scenography: the elongated pagoda, with its deep, flaring eaves, stood in an artificial lake, bracketed by the gentle arc of its access footbridges, lined with poles supporting colored glass pendants. With its bold ornamentation, rich colors, numerous bells and exaggerated roofline, the pagoda was the park's most outstanding folly. A dragon boat moored nearby completed the Hapsburg vision of Cathay.

Built of ephemeral materials, the pagoda underwent various changes at the outset of the nineteenth century and today only its foundation remains. The color scheme shown here repeats period sources.

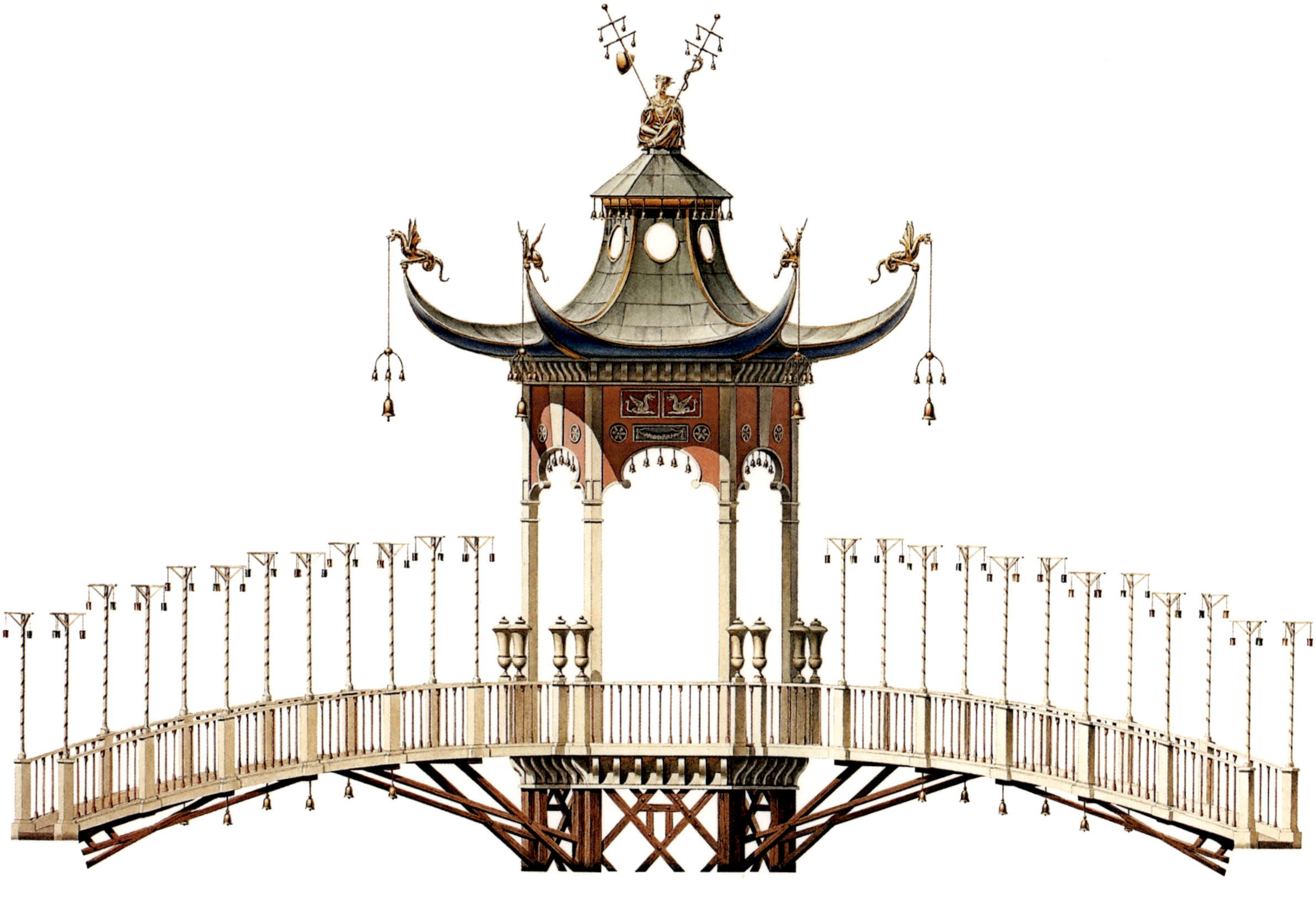

Chinese Pavilion at Cassan

Pierre-Jacques Bergeret de Grancourt, commissioner
anonymous architect
built circa 1787
extant

The pagoda at Cassan is a fiercely rare survivor, one of a mere handful among hundreds of Chinoiserie pavilions that once stood in the folly gardens of ancien régime France. More remarkable still, it is among the most handsome and architecturally accomplished as well. The pagoda was probably erected after the death of the elder Bergeret in 1785, when the son, Pierre-Jacques, confident of a vast inheritance, apparently conceived and drew plans for an ambitious English-inspired estate designed about a large artificial lake. The Chinese Pavilion, which incorporates a dam and spillway into its substructure, was the first, essential phase of this work, brought to an abrupt halt by the onset of the Revolution.

The pavilion in fact comprises two structures—a monumental stone platform upon which stands the wooden pagoda, strongly influenced by the designs of Sir William Chambers—and is typical of the period's practice of pairing widely dissimilar architectural elements to achieve picturesque effects. The classical base is notable for its sophisticated planning and vigorous ornamentation; both a stairway and a plinth, it also features a vaulted grotto in its octagonal substructure sheltering a central pool ringed by eight Greek Doric columns.

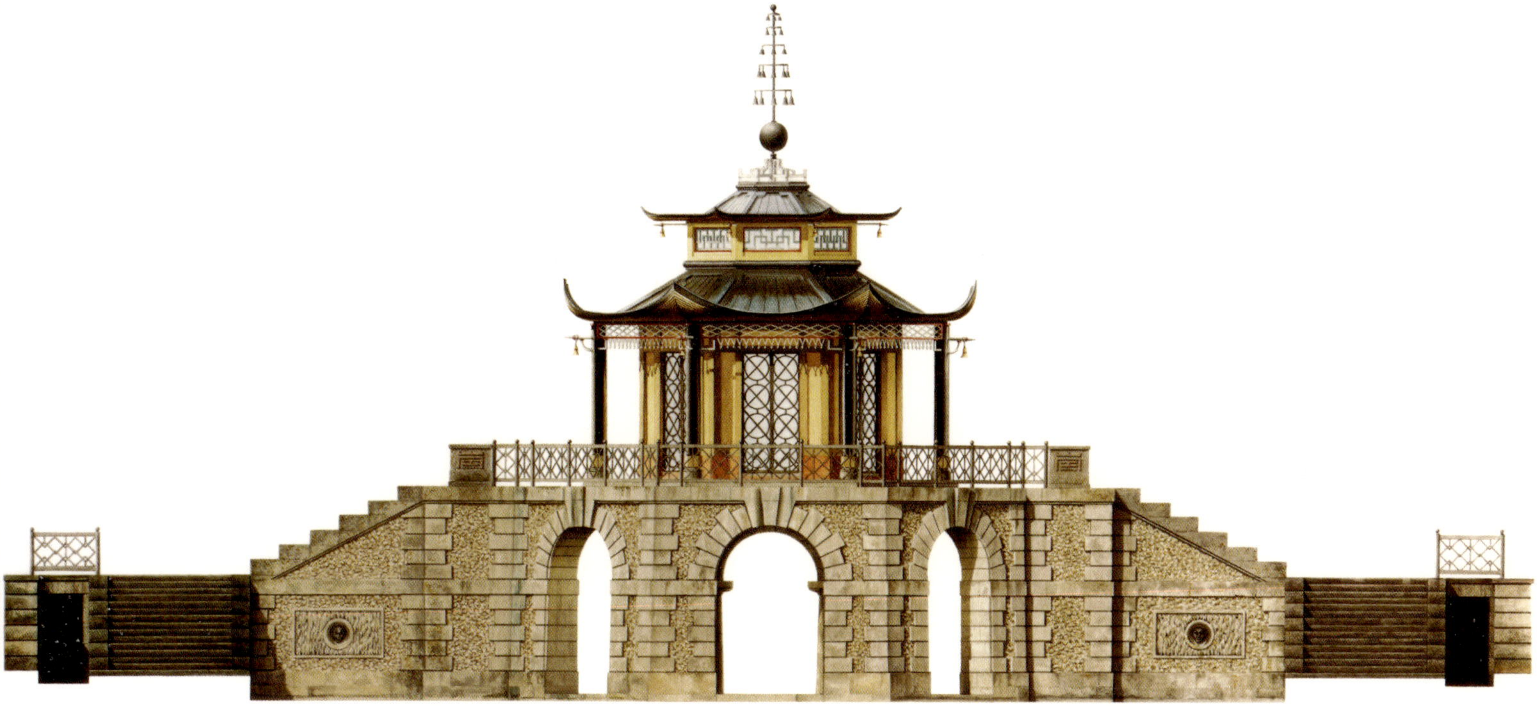

Chinese Summerhouse, Villa Doria

Orti de Raffaelo, commissioner
Francesco Bettini, architect
designed circa 1790
destroyed

The Italian architect Francesco Bettini, an intimate of the engraver Georges Le Rouge during his stay in France, became one of the most prolific garden architects in Italy upon his return to his homeland. His firsthand knowledge of the most recent developments in the art of landscaping and garden architecture, the fruit of his association with Le Rouge, helped him to secure many coveted commissions from the Italian aristocracy.

With this project for a Chinese summerhouse in the gardens of the Villa Doria in Rome, he successfully paraphrased his own prior design for a Chinoiserie dovecote intended for Attichy, France (*p. 117*). The pavilion's straightforward construction is counterbalanced by carefully placed decorative details and dramatically curving roofs. Bettini also employed his architectural trademark, the moon gate—an ancient Chinese symbol of good fortune—to enter the interior. The architect eventually fell from fashion at the end of the eighteenth century, and his theatrical creations, which delighted a generation of Italian princes, were forgotten and destroyed, leaving few traces of a prolific career.

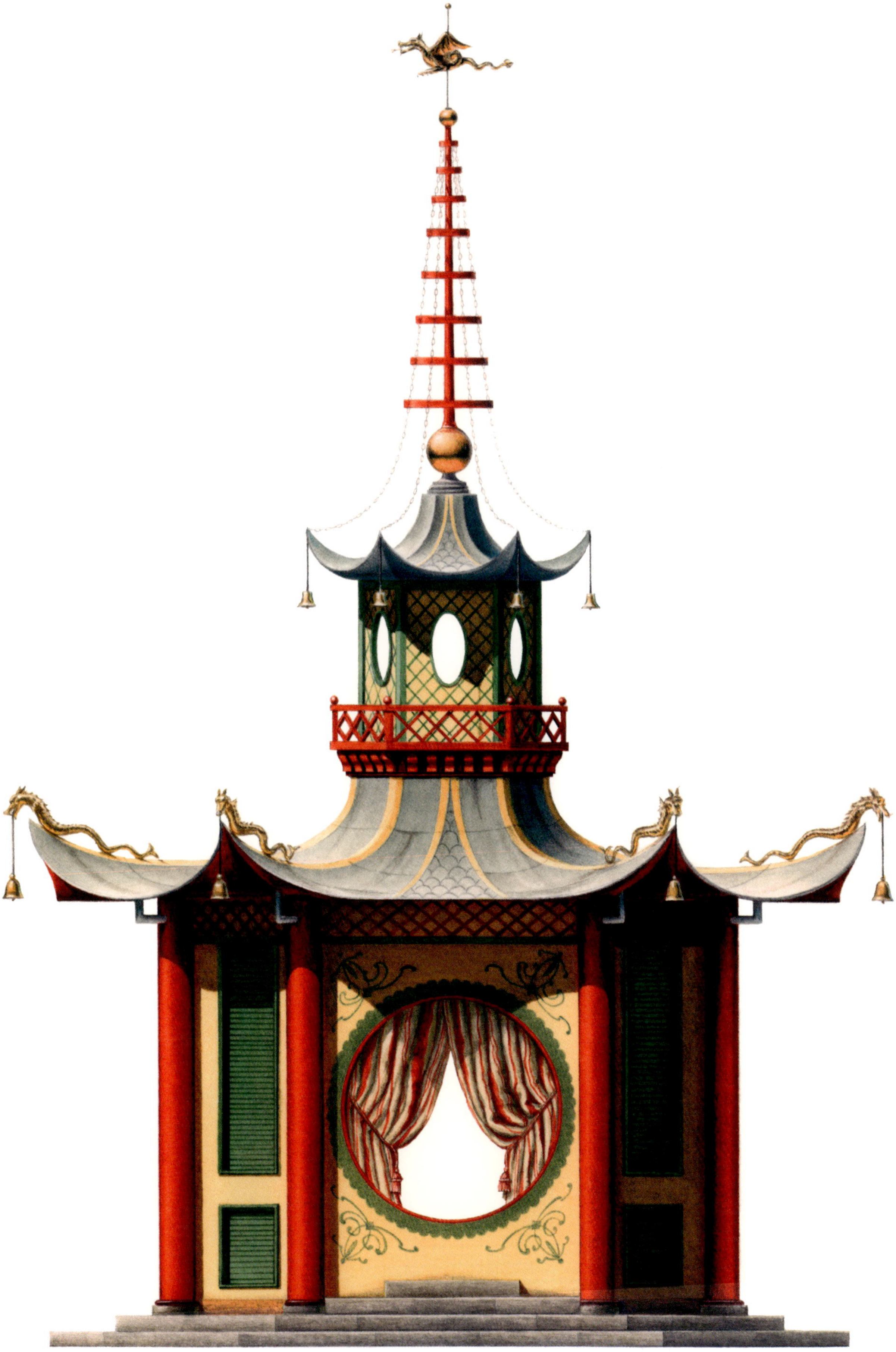

*The Chinese consider nature as their model
and they strive to imitate it with all its irregularities.*

Sir William Chambers

*"Les XI Principales Maisons de l'empereur de la Chine,"
from Georges Le Rouge's fourteenth album.*

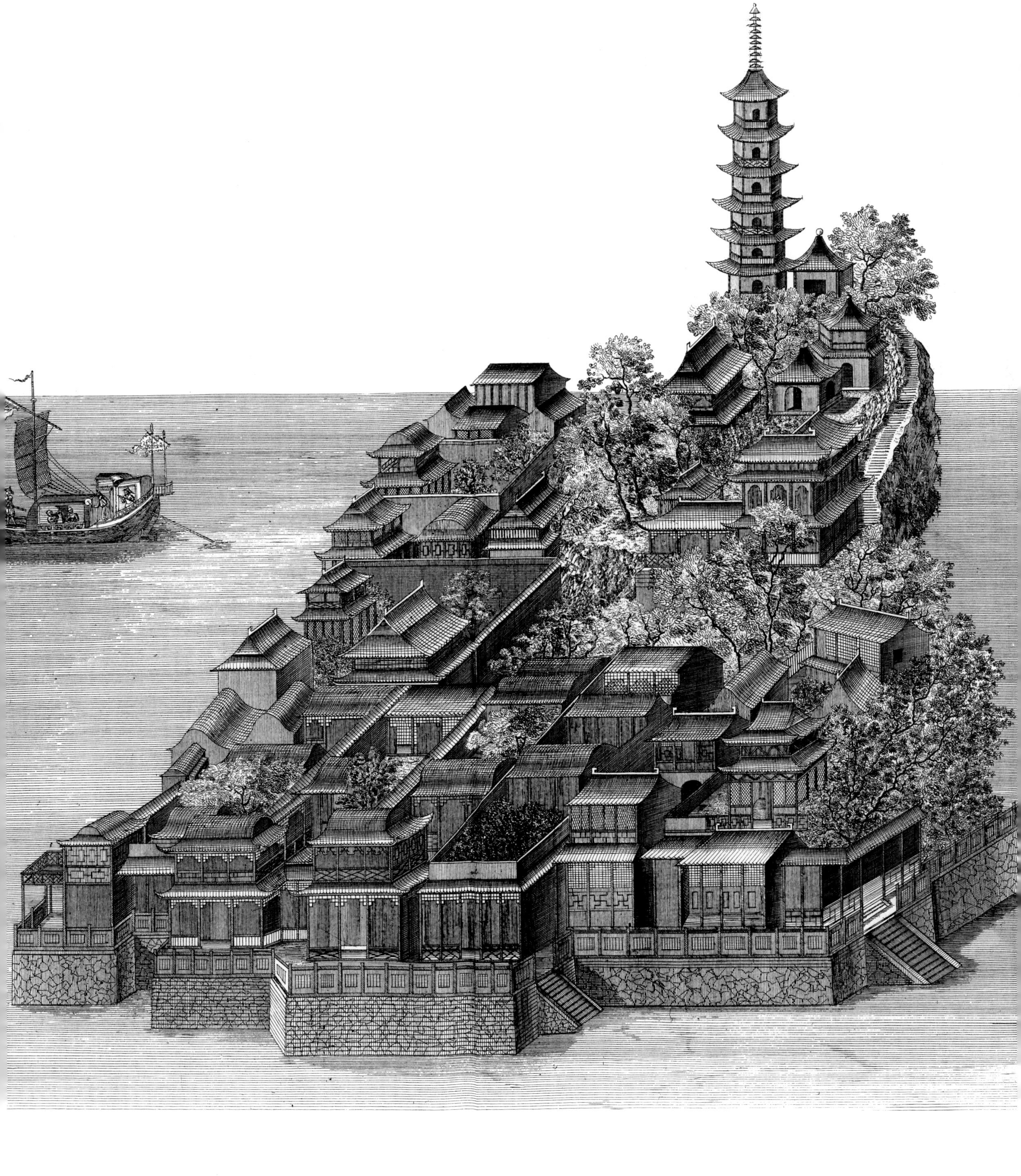

Japanese House at Paretz

Friedrich Wilhelm III of Prussia, commissioner
David and Friedrich Gilly, architects
built circa 1798
destroyed

The royal estate of Paretz, some thirteen miles from Potsdam, was daringly avant-garde; upon completion of the *Schloss* in 1797, King Friedrich Wilhelm III teased his architects by remarking that they had built for a poor country farmer, but they had in fact created a masterpiece—a *Gesamtkunstwerk* capturing the romantic sensibilities of the age. However, even at this late date no princely garden in the German states, which were forever lagging behind developments in France, was complete without a pagoda. The one at Paretz—a delicate mélange of late rococo and emerging neoclassical styles—is a reprise of David Gilly's own design for the pagoda at Steinhöffel, built for the Hofmarschall Valentin von Massow (*p. 64*).

The rustic base, a stylized grotto of fieldstone boulders, created an elevated platform for the foursquare wooden belvedere set atop it. Large window panels and a clerestory of stained glass enliven the structure's simple octagonal mass, as does the dramatic flat-sloping, rainbow-striped roof, its form reminiscent of a coolie's hat. The pagoda's color scheme is historically accurate, and its trompe l'oeil decoration announces the sober neoclassical tendencies of the period; contemporaries judged the aesthetic result Japanese. Unlike many follies that stood unused, the pavilion was a favored haunt of the royal family, who spent summer afternoons hailing passersby on the nearby country road.

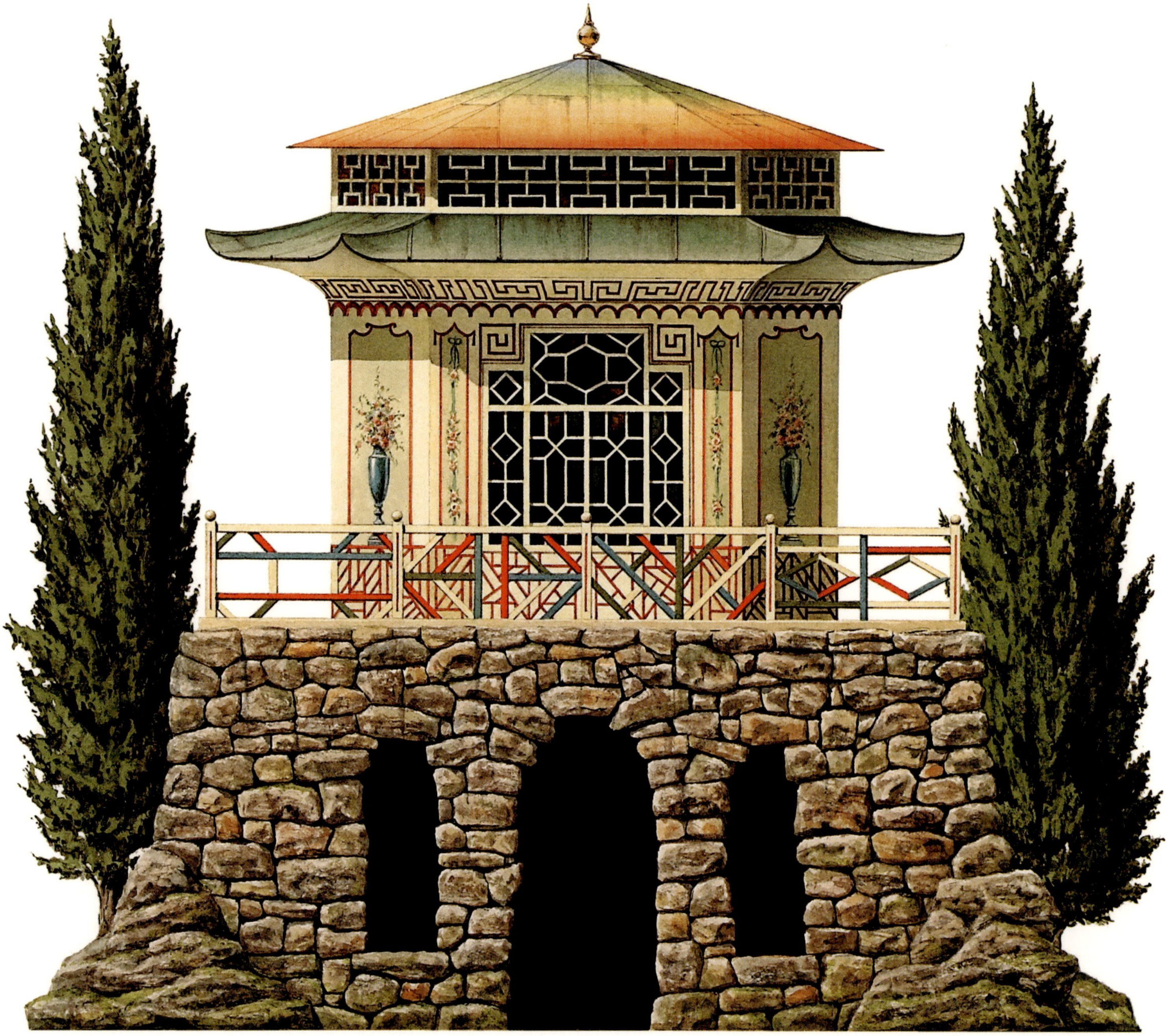

Pagoda at the Treuttelscher Garden

D. Würtz, commissioner and architect
built circa 1798
destroyed

The pagoda at the Treuttelscher Garden in Strasbourg is certainly one of the most picturesque Chinoiserie structures to be erected at the end of the eighteenth century. Built of wood and lattice with a base painted in trompe-l'oeil brickwork, its eight lacquered palm trees supported a balcony reached by a steep wooden stair behind the building. Its color scheme follows the Chinoiserie template of red, green and yellow and its ornamentation reflects the period's indifference to authentic Chinese architectural details. The pagoda's Gothic door and window frames were inscribed with sinuous signs and half-moons evoking the mysterious East, and a mandarin sat perched precariously atop its deeply flaring, scalloped roof.

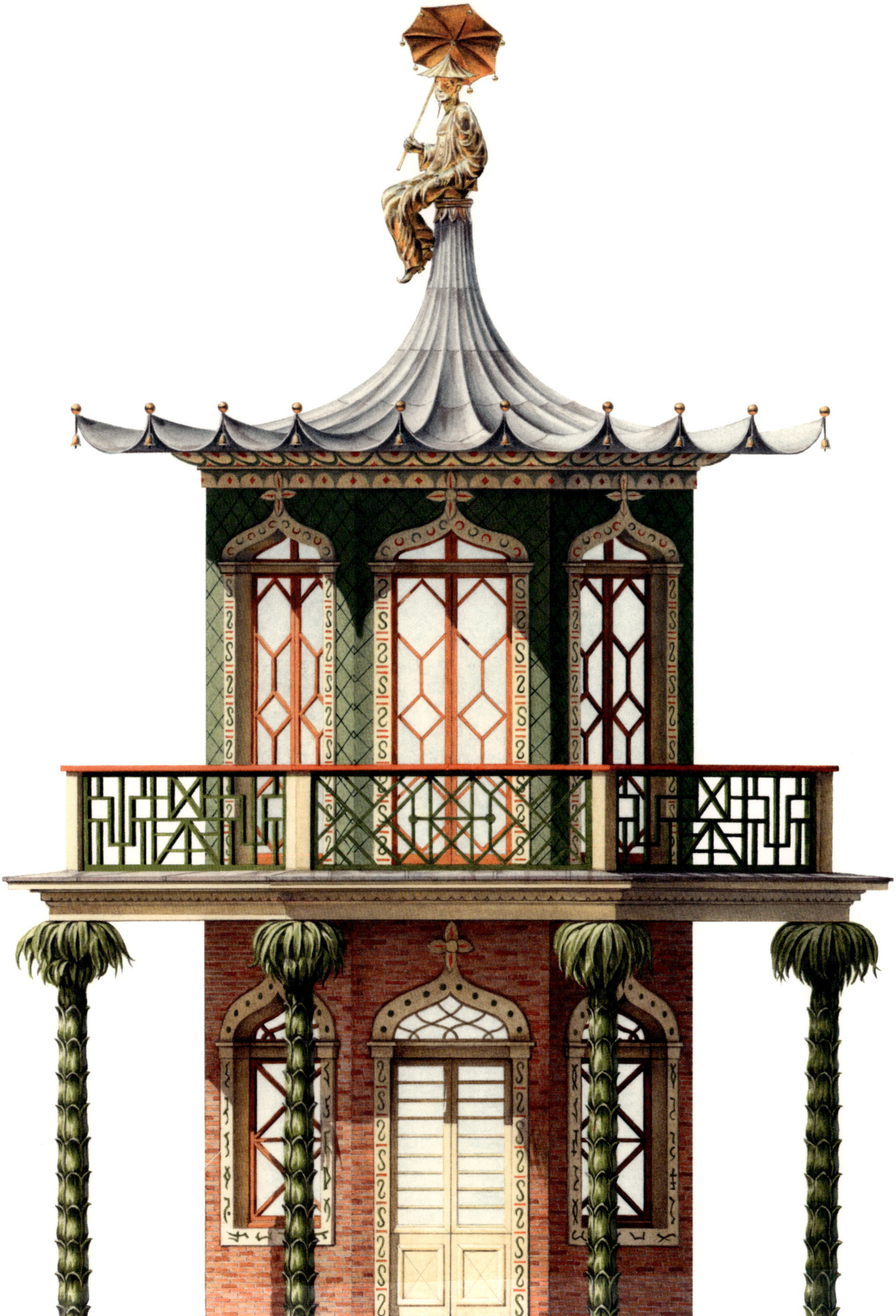

Chinese Bridge Design

Wilhelm Gottlieb Becker, publisher
designed circa 1799
unrealized design

By the close of the eighteenth century, the craze for Chinoiserie garden pavilions had reached a burgeoning European middle class eager to imitate aristocratic pretensions. True to their countrymen's organizational impulse, German publishers categorized the different styles of Chinoiserie architecture in voluminous pattern books replete with detailed descriptions of dimensions, materials and color schemes. These manuals satisfied the Germanic sense for order and afforded amateur gardeners and architects across Europe the opportunity to choose from a wide array of building types such as pavilions, pagodas, bird houses, gateways, benches and bridges. Since many aristocratic parks were still closed to the wider public, these pattern books were often the only means to form an educated opinion about Chinoiserie architecture, and Wilhelm Gottlieb Becker's volume, from which this trelliswork bridge design is drawn, became one of the most successful publications of its kind.

This design, with its sweeping lines, delicate fretwork and elongated kiosk straddling a Gothic arch, is the perfect point from which to view a sinuous stream running beneath. Bridges were an essential constituent of any *anglo-chinois* garden, since they combined two fundamental elements of such a landscape: water and a Chinoiserie structure near or spanning it, creating a picturesque scene thought to be at the heart of an authentic Chinese garden.

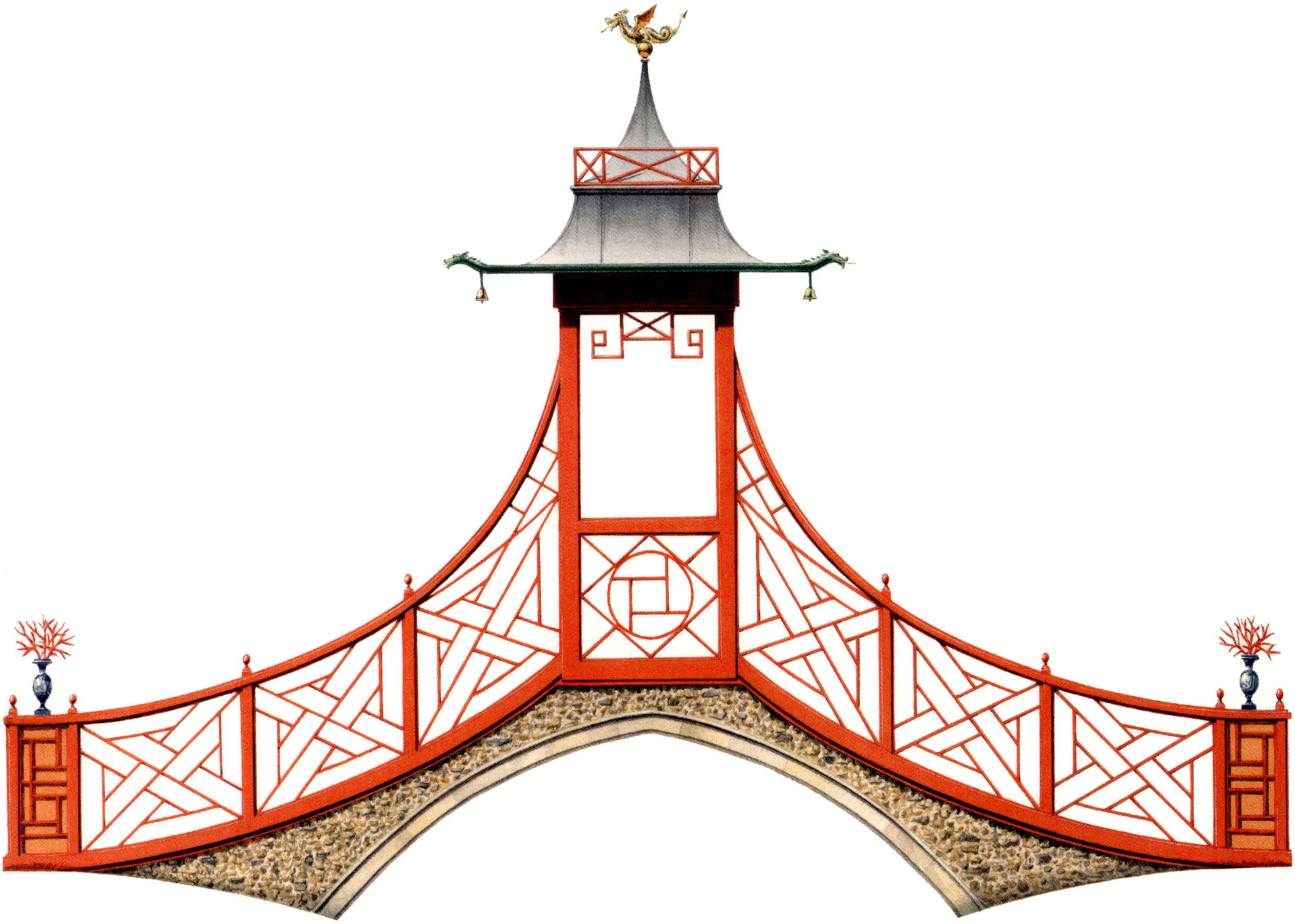

Pagoda at Rosay

Marquis de Savalète, commissioner
Jacques-Denis Antoine, architect
built 1801
extant

The pagoda at Rosay is one of only a handful of Chinoiserie pavilions remaining from hundreds built in the folly gardens of the ancien régime and in the turbulent decade following the French Revolution. The estate is itself remarkable: the park is unique in being a perfectly preserved example of an Anglo-Chinese folly garden. The handsome, moated Louis XIII château is sited on a wooded hillside overlooking a wide, open valley. The extensive gardens, redrawn at the behest of the Marquis de Savalète under the direction of the architect Jacques-Denis Antoine at the turn of the nineteenth century, features several superb neo-Palladian follies and an abundance of grottoes, rockworks and sinuous watercourses fed by springs.

The pagoda stands atop an extensive artificial grotto on axis with the château on the site of the earlier formal parterre and is reached by an arching iron bridge, a picturesque mise-en-scène recalling pagodas at Bagatelle (*p. 87*) and Bonnelles (*p. 121*). Its delicate details—elongated Corinthian colonnettes, scallop-shell frieze and faux-painted brickwork—make it a Directoire interpretation of the Philosopher's Pavilion at Bagatelle, also based on a hexagonal plan.

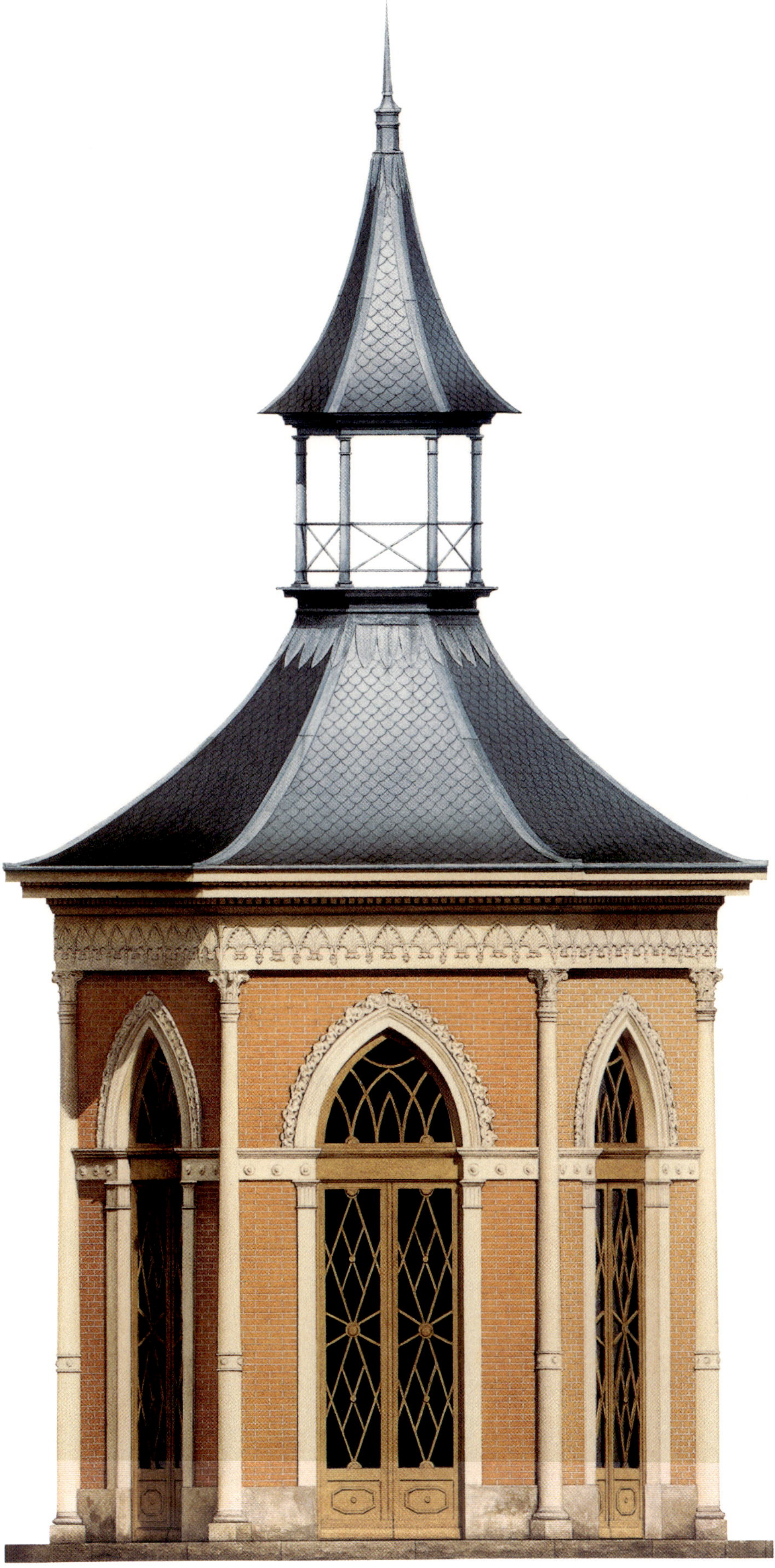

Musician's Pagoda at the Mall, Central Park

Frederick Law Olmsted, park superintendent

Jacob Wrey Mould, architect

built 1862

destroyed 1922

Once known fondly to New Yorkers as "the Old Bandstand," the Musician's Pagoda was one of Central Park's most familiar landmarks and the focal point of civic life on the Mall from the post-Civil War era until the promise of the Naumburg Bandshell precipitated its destruction in 1922. Frederick Law Olmsted, the park's designer and first superintendent, originally envisioned a floating music pavilion moored in the lake near Bethesda Terrace, but dismissed the idea in favor of a prominent site on the Mall promenade.

Jacob Wrey Mould's initial design for the floating cast-iron pavilion, hardly altered in execution, was incontestably his most outlandish design for the park. The hexagonally planned pagoda featured eclectic but predominantly Moorish details and was clothed in what Mould vaunted as a "hell of color"—a folly in the truest sense and an unexpected touch of Oriental opulence in nineteenth-century Manhattan. The color scheme is historically accurate.

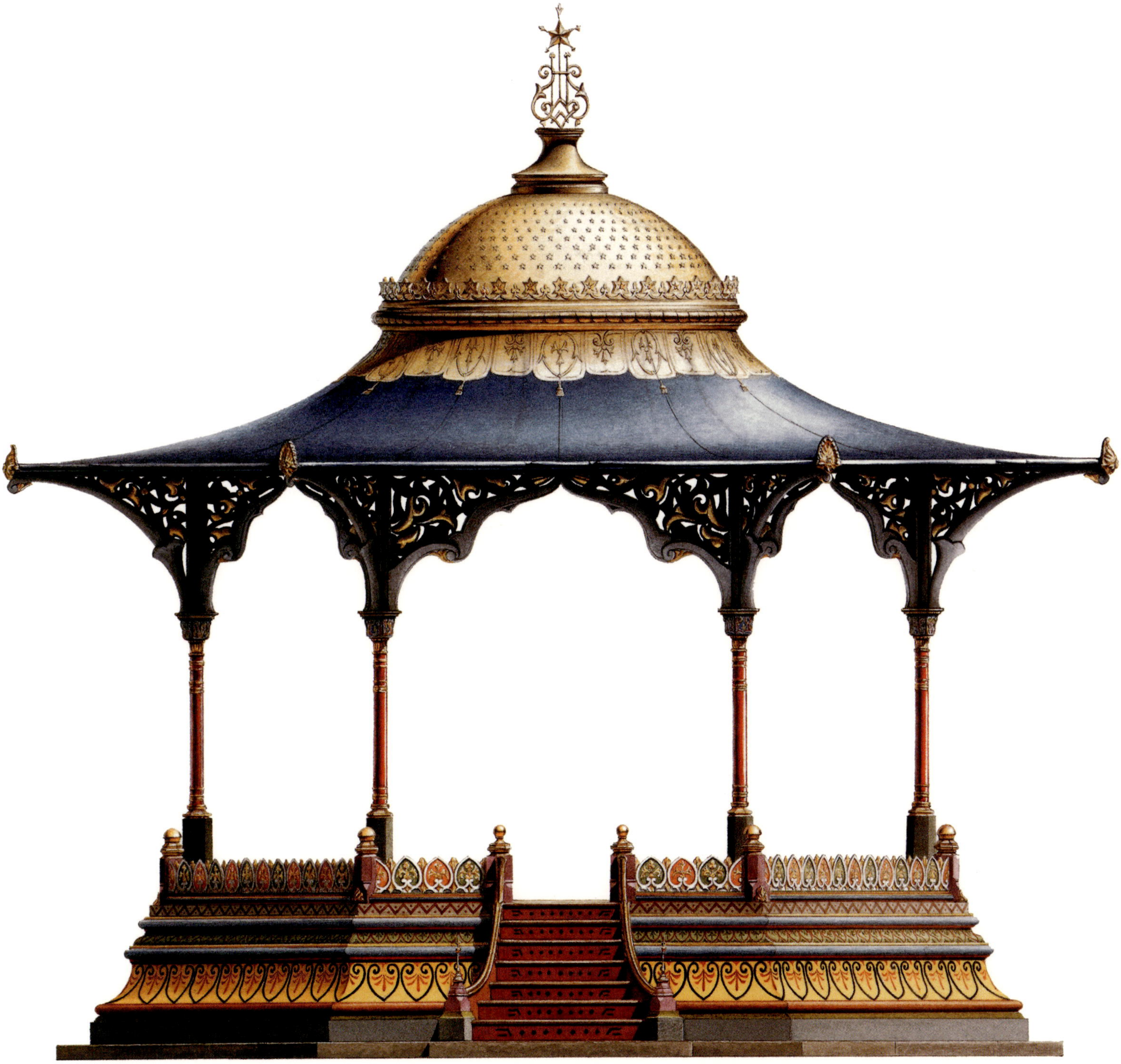

SELECTED BIBLIOGRAPHY

Argenville, Dezallier d'. *Theorie and Practice of Gardening.* London, 1728.

Belevitch-Stankevitch, Henri. *Le goût chinois en France au temps de Louis XIV.* Geneva, 1970.

Blaikie, Thomas. *The Diary of a Scotch Gardener at the French Court.* London, 1931.

Blaser, Werner. *Chinesische Pavillon Architektur.* Niederteufen, 1974.

Brunel, Georges. *Pagodes et Dragons: Exoticisme et fantaisie dans l'Europe rococo, 1720–1770.* Paris, 2007.

Carrogis, Louis, alias Carmontelle. *Le jardin de Monceau.* Paris, 1779.

Castiglione, Guiseppe. *Palaces, Pavilions and Gardens* [engravings]. Paris, 1978 (1738–1786).

Cerutti, Joseph-Antoine. *Les jardins de Betz.* Paris, 1792.

Chambers, Sir William. *Designs of Chinese buildings, furniture, dresses, machines, and utensils, etc.* London, 1757.

_____. *A Dissertation on Oriental Gardening.* London, 1772.

_____. *Plans, elevations, sections and perspective views of gardens and buildings at Kew in Surrey.* London, 1763.

Chang, Sheng-Ching. *Natur und Landschaft: Der Einfluss von Athanasius Kirchners "China Illustrata."* Berlin, 2003.

Chiu, Che Bing. *Yuanming Yuan: Le Jardin de la Clarté Parfaite.* Paris, 2000.

Conner, Patrick. *Oriental Architecture in the West.* London, 1973.

Dams, Bernd H., and Zega, Andrew. *Pleasure Pavilions and Follies.* Paris, 1995.

De Bagatelle à Monceau, 1778–1978. Exhibition catalogue. Paris, 1978.

du Halde, Jean Baptiste. *Description géographique, historique, etc. de l'empire de la Chine…* Paris, 1741.

Erdberg, Eleonor von. *Chinese Influence on European Garden Structures.* Cambridge, MA, 1936.

Erlach, Johann Bernard Fischer von. *Entwurf einer historischen Architektur.* Leipzig, 1752.

Giersberg, Hans-Joachim. *Das Chinesische Haus im Park von Sanssouci.* Berlin, 1993.

Girardin, René de. *De la composition des paysages.* Paris, 1777.

Halfpenny, William, and John. *Rural Architecture in the Chinese Taste.* New York, 1968 (London, 1752).

Harcourt, François d' (Ganay, Ernest de, ed.). *Traité de la décoration des dehors, des jardins et des parcs.* Paris, 1919.

Héré de Corny, Emmanuel. *Recueil des plans, élévations et coupes…que le Roi de Pologne occupe en Lorraine.* 2 vols. Paris, 1753–1756.

Hirschfeld, C.C.L. *Theorie der Gartenkunst*. 5 vols. Leipzig, 1779–1785.

Honour, Hugh. *Chinoiseries: The Vision of Cathay*. New York, 1962.

Jackson, Anna, and Jaffer, Amin, eds. *Encounters: The Meeting of Asia and Europe—1500–1800*. London, 2004.

Jacobson, Dawn. *Chinoiseries*. London, 1993.

Jarry, Madeleine. *Chinoiseries*. Fribourg, 1981.

Kirchner, Athanasius. *China monumentis qua sacris qua profanes, illustrata*. Amsterdam, 1672.

Koppelkamm, Stefan. *Der Imaginäre Orient*. Berlin, 1987.

Krafft, Johann Karl. *Plans des plus beaux jardins pittoresques de France, d'Angleterre, et d'Allemagne*. 2 vols. Paris, 1809-1810.

Laborde, Alexandre de. *Descriptions des nouveaux jardins pittoresques de la France et de ses anciens châteaux*. Paris, 1808.

Laske. F. *Der Ostasiatische Einfluss auf die Baukunst des Abendlandes*. Berlin, 1909.

Le Rouge, Georges. *Détail des nouveaux jardins à la mode...* Paris, 2004 (1774–1789).

Ligne, Charles-Joseph, Prince de. *Coup d'œil sur Beloeil*. Berkeley, 1991 (Paris, 1781).

McGill, Forrest, ed. *A Curious Affair: The Fascination Between East and West*. San Francisco, 2006.

Mignini, Filippo. *Matteo Ricci: Europa am Hof der Ming*. Berlin, 2005.

Morel, Jean. *Théorie des jardins; ou l'art des jardins de la Nature*. Paris, 1776.

Nieuhoff, Johann. *Het gezandschap der Neerlandtsche Oost-Indische Compagnie*. London, 1669.

Rawski, Evelyn S., and Rawson, Jessica, eds. *China: The Three Emperors*. London, 2006.

Reichwein, Adolf. *China und Europa*. Berlin, 1923.

Rivière, Mercier de la. *L'ordre naturel et essentiel des sociétés politiques*. Paris, 1767.

Rousseau, Jean-Jacques. *Julie, ou, la nouvelle Héloïse*. 4 vols. Paris, 1928 (1761).

Setterwall, Ake. *The Chinese Pavilion at Drottningholm*. Malmo, 1974.

Siren, Osvald. *China and Gardens of Europe of the Eighteenth Century*. Washington, DC, 1990.

Sperlich, Martin, and Börsch-Supran, Helmut, et al. *China und Europa*. Berlin, 1973.

Temple, Sir William. *Upon the Gardens of Epicurus*. London, 1908 (1685).

Valder, Peter. *Gardens in China*. Portland, 2002.

Voltaire, François-Marie Arouet. *The Complete Works*. 135 vols. Geneva, Banbury, Oxford, 1968.

Walpole, Horace. *On Modern Gardening*. London, 1780.

Watelet, Claude-Henri. *Essai sur les jardins*. Paris, 2004 (1774).

Whatley, Thomas. *Observations on Modern Gardening*. London, 1770.

ILLUSTRATION CREDITS

All the elevations of buildings illustrating this book are reproduced from original watercolors by Edward Andrew Zega and Bernd H. Dams, protected under the copyright laws of the United States. They may not be reproduced in any form or by any means without the express written permission of the artists: *pp. 7, 31, 33, 35, 37, 39, 41, 45, 47, 49, 51, 53, 71, 73, 75, 77, 79, 83, 85, 87, 89, 91, 107, 109, 111, 113, 115, 117, 121, 123, 125, 127, 129, 139, 141, 143, 145, 147, 151, 153, 155, 157, 159.*

Photography of the authors' watercolors: *pp. 7, 31, 33, 37, 39, 41, 45, 47, 49, 51, 53, 71, 73, 89, 91, 107, 109, 111, 113, 117, 123, 125, 143, 151, 157, 159* © Philippe Sébert, Paris. All other photography of the authors' watercolors: © Edward Andrew Zega and Bernd H. Dams.

Bibliothèque du Musée de l'Opéra de Paris: *p. 8.*

Albertina Museum, Vienna: *pp. 14-15.*

Staatliche Museen Preussischer Kulturbesitz, Berlin: *pp. 21, 22.*

The Getty Research Institute/The Getty Center, Los Angeles: *p. 26.*

Musée des Beaux-Arts et d'Archéologie, Besançon: *p. 43.*

Courtesy picture archive Philip Wilson Publisher Ltd., London: *pp. 54-55.*

Museum Schloss Augustusburg, Brühl: *p. 60.*

The Princes' Czartoryski Foundation, National Museum, Krakow: *p. 63.*

Graphisches Kabinett der Stiftung Moritzburg, Halle: *p. 64.*

École Nationale Supérieure des Beaux-Arts, Paris: *pp. 66, 163.*

Private collection, Paris (photography © Philippe Sébert, Paris): *pp. 80-81.*

The Yale Center for British Art, Paul Mellon Collection, courtesy The Bridgeman Art Library, Paris: *pp. 92-93.*

Musée du Louvre, Paris, courtesy Agence Photo Réunion des Musées Nationaux: *pp. 130-131.*

Opposite: Cartouche Evoking China, *engraved by Benedikt Winckler after Jacques Lajoue.*

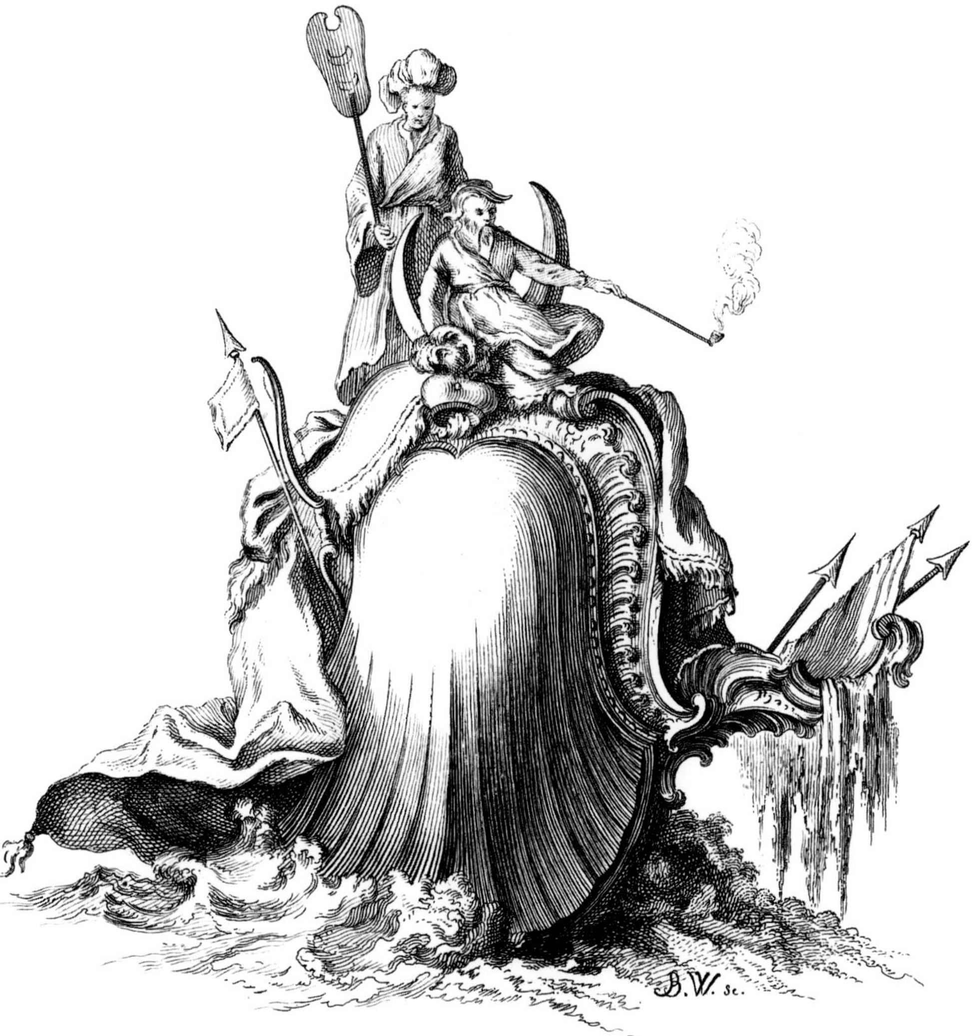
B.W. sc.